# Secret[s of]
# Relationship
# Success

## Strategies for lasting happiness

## Vanessa Lloyd Platt

**Vermilion**
**LONDON**

5 7 9 10 8 6 4

First published in the United Kingdom in 2000 by Vermilion
an imprint of Ebury Press
The Random House Group Ltd.
Random House, 20 Vauxhall Bridge Road, London SW1V 2SA

Random House Australia (Pty) Limited
20 Alfred Street, Milsons Point, Sydney,
New South Wales 2061, Australia

Random House New Zealand Limited
18 Poland Road, Glenfield,
Auckland 10, New Zealand

Random House (Pty) Limited
Endulini, 5A Jubilee Road,
Parktown 2193, South Africa

The Random House Group Limited Reg. No. 954009
www.randomhouse.co.uk

A CIP catalogue record for this book is available from the British Library.

ISBN: 0 09 185624 8

Printed and bound in Great Britain by
Cox & Wyman Ltd, Reading , Berkshire

Papers used by Vermilion are natural, recyclable products
made from wood grown in sustainable forests.

Cover Illustration: Martyn Lucksford
Cover Designer: Prospero, London
Text Design: Jerry Goldie Graphic Design

# Acknowledgements

I would like to thank the following people without whom this book could not have been written;

My darling husband Daniel for his patience and understanding during the time I wrote this, who together with my wonderful sons, Michael and Gary, helped me to put balance into this book, giving sensible criticism and encouraging me to overcome my tendency to ask them what is wrong every half an hour; My loving and supporting parents, Ruth and Martin, who have always been there to encourage me; my sister Carole for her support; Kerrie Hall for typing the manuscript and amendments to this book with unflagging enthusiasm; Mary Ketley for her help in minding the practice while I wrote this; my friend Antonia Berger for being so special; my friends Rochelle and Jackie for our hilarious lunches which have helped keep me sane; my mother in law, Essie Somers for listening so intently to my ideas; my editor Fiona MacIntyre for her tireless energy in editing this book and for giving me that chance to write it. Derek Webster for changing my view of life; Susan Watkins, Marisa Rueda and Marta Rodriguez for writing the only book on feminism I could ever understand, my friend Harvey; I have felt your presence throughout the time I was writing this; you will always be in our hearts and never forgotten. Last but not least I would like to thank all of my clients, past and present for their stories which have made this book.

*This book is dedicated
to my darling husband Daniel,
and my sons Michael and Gary.*

# Contents

# Introduction

Are you alone, having recently been left by your boyfriend or husband, wondering where it all went wrong and how you might win him back? Or are you about to embark on a new relationship, and desperate not to fall into the same traps again? Then read on!

This book attempts to identify the problems that exist between men and women today and presents practical solutions for dealing with them. It also highlights complaints most often made by men about women that can lead to a relationship's demise – which no wife or girlfriend can afford to ignore.

As a woman who has been a divorce lawyer for over twenty years, I have observed patterns of behaviour being repeated time and time again, and I have come to the conclusion that, in most cases, it is women who are responsible for the majority of the dissatisfaction being experienced today in male-female relationships. Too often, in divorce proceedings, I observe the Dragon Woman, whose conduct is bound to exterminate any relationship in which she is involved, and the counterpart she has created, Colditz Man, who cannot wait to plot his escape from her.

With increasing frequency, particularly during the last five years, men from all walks of life who are divorcing their wives have begun complaining to me about what they perceive as women's uncontrolled aggression in their relationships. They claim that women have changed beyond recognition. From being soft, compliant and loving, they have become volatile, hard and distant. They claim that women seem more and more unable to balance working outside the home with their relationships so that home for everyone has now become a battleground. It appears that many women are fighting so hard for equality in relationships, as well as the workplace, that men are running for cover. Contrary to what many modern women seem to believe, partnership is not necessarily synonymous with equality.

That is, many partnerships work exceedingly well which are not entirely equal. These relationships accommodate the strengths and weaknesses of the individuals involved, with each half of the couple giving the other support. This is how marriage used to work. So why is it not working for many people today?

An article I wrote for the *Daily Mail* in February, 2000, expressed my view that women are to blame for the world's escalating divorce rate. And so this book was born, in which I explain how I came to that conclusion, and how women who exhibit certain fire-breathing traits and men who feel they are in Colditz Prison may alter their behaviour so that their marriages and relationships may be saved… and flourish.

# CHAPTER 1

# Why Dragon Women Are to Blame

*If you really want to know, I am really tired of*
*feminists, sick of them. They have really dug*
*themselves into their own grave. Any man would be a*
*fool who didn't agree with equal rights and pay, but*
*some women, now juggling with career, lover,*
*children, wifehood have spread themselves too thin*
*and are very unhappy.*

– Michael Douglas (actor)

As a divorce lawyer, I constantly hear clients – men *and* women – complaining about their partner's unacceptable behaviour. Repeatedly, and with increasing frequency over the twenty years I have been in practice, they describe the same types of behaviour, often even using similar words for it.

However, a new more alarming trend – particularly noticeable in the last five years – is the number of complaints being made by men about women's conduct. This has led me to the conclusion that women's behaviour has undergone a revolution that men simply cannot tolerate.

This behaviour seems to be causing the breakdown of relationships in Britain, which now has the highest divorce rate anywhere, with the rest of the world close on its heels, not to mention the fact that more couples are choosing to co-habit (live together) than ever before. Statistics show that these relationships are four times more likely to end than marriages. To say that society now has a huge relationship problem which affects us all would be an understatement.

So what is this behaviour that men are complaining about? It includes:

- Body language so hostile that it screams, 'Get lost!'
- Rudeness in which women are increasingly unwilling to listen to men, often dismissing their opinions as valueless.
- Repeated shouting matches in which unfounded or vitriolic accusations are levelled at them by women.
- An insistence that women are right, leaving no room for discussion.
- Criticism and unrealistic demands; women are not just nags but character-demolishers.
- Women behaving like men in the workplace and at home.
- Women dressing like men and trying to emulate them.
- The disappearance of qualities like softness and gentleness in women. Men wonder what happened to femininity.

Of course, speaking as a woman, it is difficult to believe that women could be seen in such a light. But this is how men perceive us, and we must deal with it if we want to have husbands or boyfriends at all. So I have devised a name to describe this persona. She exemplifies the kind of woman no red-blooded, ordinary male wants to be anywhere near. (I'm not sure I want to be anywhere around her myself!) I have called her 'Dragon Woman'. In her most extreme form, she is the kind of person who is intolerable to men, and probably, if truth be known, also to herself. She will blithely and unknowingly exterminate any relationship she has by breathing fire over it. (If you recognise fire-breathing tendencies in yourself, then you must act now to repair the damage you have already done or face the inevitable consequences of a broken relationship with all the attendant pain that it will bring you.)

> *Men are not worried by things but by their ideas about things. When we meet with difficulties, become anxious or troubled, let us not blame others but rather ourselves, that is, our ideas about things.*
> – Epictetus

This is not the only problem, however. Dragon Women are creating a male counterpart. I call him 'Colditz Man' – he constantly plots his escape from any relationship he has, particularly with or as a result of his involvement with Dragon Women.

But husbands and boyfriends who recognise themselves in this role should take heart. There may be a way forward. Strategically placing this book on your bedside table may well do the trick. Once your wife or girlfriend implements its suggestions, you won't need to escape, and, indeed, will not want to. This book will inspire the ideal post-feminist woman and man – people who truly understand the needs of their mates while fulfilling their own. I hope it will similarly inspire the ideal post-feminist man.

Instead of the kind of person I term Dragon Woman – the dragon of European myth which is all that is evil and bad in human nature (always portrayed as being killed by Saint George or the archangel Michael) – your love will emerge like a butterfly to become a dragon of good fortune. With your help, she can learn to turn her fire towards things that will benefit the world, and to warm you rather than burn you to a crisp.

If you, as a man, do not help her refocus her fiery attention upon things that matter and are useful, she risks becoming a shrivelled wretch of a fallible human being, having turned her flames upon those she loves and, at the same time, upon herself.

For when you breathe fire over those you love, you also burn yourself. If you express love to others and know how to do so, then love will come to you. This, as the Bible and many of the world's religious stories and mythologies illustrate, is the crux of our problem as human beings.

It is one that humanity must solve if we are to heal rather than destroy ourselves and our world. If we resolve this, preferably on a global scale, I believe that relationships will flourish once again and the future of civilised society will be secured.

> *A woman is not needed to do a man's work. She is not needed to think man's thoughts. Her mission is not to enhance the masculine spirit, but to express the feminine. Hers is not to preserve a man-made world, but to create a human world by the infusion of the feminine element into all of its activities.*
>
> – Margaret Sanger (1879–1996)

So who is Dragon Woman? She is someone who has become aggressive, volatile, hard and distant, particularly in her relationships with men. A Dragon Woman believes that men are from Mars and should stay there!

> *New York City has finally hired women to pick up the garbage which makes sense to me, since, as I have discovered, a good bit of being a woman consists of picking up garbage.*
>
> – Anna Quindlen

# Dragon Woman Types

There are many different colonies of Dragon Women. A few examples follow which illustrate the qualities and characteristics which men find least tantalising in women and will ensure the creation of legions of Colditz Men.

## Dragon Girls

Young women aged between 16 and 20, many of whom believe that boys and men are a complete waste of space, have grown up in the post-feminist world and the era of Girlpower. Their gospel is that girls are all-powerful, should have total control and do not necessarily need males at all. This distorted message was aimed by pop record moguls at impressionable young girls and enforced a powerful belief which can only lead to disastrous future relationships.

*Marrying a man is like buying something you have been admiring for a long time in a shop window. You may love it when you get it home, but it doesn't always go with everything else.*

– Jean Kerr

## Dragonettes

Working women between 20 and 30, who are termed 'ladettes' by the press, believe that they are like men and can behave as outrageously as 'the lads'. A typical ladette dresses in 'hard clothes', not necessarily to attract men. She goes out drinking after work and may burp, belch or break wind without embarrassment. She is one of the lads, game for anything – particularly wild, destructive behaviour. She has forgotten, in her quest to be like a man, that men and women are very different, both physiologically and mentally.

## Dragon Drones

These are the ranks of hardworking married and single women who have fought so hard for equality in the workplace that they continue the fight at home. Men think they are overtly hostile and aggressive and blame men for all their problems. Dragon Drones cannot stop working or fighting for their rights and are oblivious to the chaos they cause around them.

## Dragon Hunters

These are women who carry an aura of desperation and self-loathing about them and display inappropriate behaviour in social gatherings. Their attempts to attract men only repel them. They may be divorcees or unmarried women who are desperate to find husbands.

## Dragon Spiters

Divorced or single women who, embittered by their experiences, have turned into man-haters.

## Dragon Bullies

Married women who, from feelings of inferiority and insecurity, aggressively try to assert themselves by bullying anyone they can easily intimidate, particularly men.

## Dragon Spinsters

Embittered, unmarried man-haters who have never mastered the art of male-female relationships and despise any woman who is in a happy relationship.

*The male function is to produce sperm. We now have sperm banks.*

– Valerie Solanas

There are, of course, many women who do not display these characteristics and have perfectly happy relationships. Regrettably, the numbers that do show them are increasing rapidly.

Some women who have striven for and achieved success at work are starting to believe that men are of little or no use to them, and that male-female relationships are of transitional benefit only (e.g., for sexual gratification or to produce offspring). The concepts of love, respect and companionship seem to have no part in their lives because they believe that if they allow themselves to be vulnerable, they will somehow lose out. Subconsciously, these women deny themselves any chance of a lasting or permanent relationship.

> *A woman needs a man like a fish needs a bicycle.*
> – Gloria Steinem

This attitude is a step beyond the views of the early feminist Mary Wolstonecraft, who said that she 'did not wish for women to have power over men but over themselves'. Some women today have begun to perceive themselves as being in control of society and men as objects of ridicule.

> *Women want mediocre men and men are willing to be as mediocre as possible.*
> – Margaret Mead

Having dealt with many women like this, I realise that their superficial aggression hides an inner insecurity. They crave the warmth of a loving relationship, but have no notion of how to achieve it. It is to those women in particular that I address this book.

> *There is no greater risk perhaps than matrimony, but there is nothing happier than a happy marriage.*
> – Benjamin Disraeli

Men today find themselves in a confused and changing world. They have no idea how to deal with Dragon Women or what contemporary women expect from them. Dragon Women bring home with them the same aggression they display in the office. Dragon Women's aggressiveness is emasculating men, who are developing worrying physical and mental problems.

In recent years, there has been a substantial increase in mental illness, particularly in young men, and in alcohol, drug and nicotine addiction. The suicide rate among young men has never been higher. Stress-induced illnesses such as irritable bowel syndrome, stomach ulcers, high blood pressure and coronary artery disease have also risen alarmingly, as have the rates of impotency and premature balding. These symptoms cannot be explained away as merely the result of diet, pollution or work-related stress.

Recent surveys show that men's sperm count is falling rapidly worldwide, particularly in Britain. According to these surveys, it is not just the increase in female hormones in men which is affecting their sperm count, but the stress caused by the impact of women's changing role in society. Research carried out in 1992 found that men's fertility was dropping by 3.7 per cent a year.

In her latest book, *The Whole Woman*, Germaine Greer claims that 'nobody knows what is going on'. My own view is that men are being made to feel useless and are beginning to evolve in a different way physiologically. If we want to ensure the survival of the species, we cannot afford to ignore this possibility. Do we really want men to degenerate into short, balding, infertile, acid-producing specimens suffering from heart disease, alcoholism and other problems in their twenties?

*Husbands are like fires; they go out if unattended.*
– Zsa Zsa Gabor

What Dragon Women have created is an unhappy partner who doesn't want a constant battle for control or superiority. Colditz Man wants peace and to enjoy life. Denied this, he will have an affair to obtain peace, affection and solace, or simply leave and instigate separation or divorce proceedings.

It is unreasonable for women to continue to blame men for all the ills of society. Women's current stance regarding men is causing major relationship rifts and women must rethink their attitudes.

The following examples, drawn from some cases in which I have been involved, illustrate the problems many couples are dealing with today. They show all too clearly that men are facing Dragon Women who generally fail to grasp the situation until it is too late.

> *The trouble with some women is that they get all excited about nothing and then marry him.*
>
> – Cher

**CASE STUDY** ••••••••••••••

Samantha married Jack when she was 21. When they met, she was sweet, helpful and very supportive of Jack. By the age of 27, Samantha had changed beyond recognition. She was now working in marketing and Jack felt that she treated him with little or no respect. She surrounded herself with 'ladette' friends, with whom she would regularly go for a drink after work. She rarely shared a meal with Jack, or communicated with him at all, in the evenings. He complained that she would speak endlessly on the telephone to her friends, and, more hurtfully, talk about him in the most derogatory way. So often, he said, when he came home from work, he would hear her screaming to her friend down the phone, 'Oh Superwimp has just walked in'.

Jack coped with this treatment for two more years. Then one day he met Jenny, who was reassuring and warm towards him.

When he left home, Samantha was distraught. 'After all I did for him,' she said, 'he ran off with someone else. Well, that's men for you.'

● ● ● ● ● ● ● ● ● ● ● ● ● ● ● ● ● ● ● ● ● ●

*When God made man, she was only testing.*
                                        – Graffiti in London, W11

**CASE STUDY** ● ● ● ● ● ● ● ● ● ● ● ● ● ●

Cynthia moved in with Jerry after they had been going out for about three months. Jerry wanted them to live together for a while, and was very much in favour of marriage. At 24, Cynthia felt that she was ready to live with someone but unsure about marriage. They bought a home together and pooled their resources. On the third day after they had started living together, Cynthia pinned a list on the bedroom wall headed: 'Your tasks or be damned'. The list included hoovering, washing, ironing, cooking, good sex and paying for evenings out. When Jerry asked Cynthia whether this was a joke, she said, 'No. This is what men expect of women, so why shouldn't we expect it of men?' Cynthia made it clear to Jerry that she didn't really need a man at all but thought that it might be useful to have some assistance and had felt that pooling their resources would be helpful.

After a few weeks, Jerry became panic-stricken because Cynthia seemed so unsharing. He sought my advice; he was devastated by Cynthia's transformation into someone so cold and calculating. He felt he simply could not continue. He said that love and affection didn't even seem to enter Cynthia's world. The house was sold and the proceeds split.

Jerry has now found happiness with a new companion, Linda, who has a more sharing approach to their relationship.

● ● ● ● ● ● ● ● ● ● ● ● ● ● ● ● ● ● ● ● ● ●

*I enjoy dating married men because they don't want
anything kinky like breakfast.*

– Joni Rodgers

**CASE STUDY** ✴✴✴✴✴✴✴✴✴✴✴✴✴✴

Sue and Sheldon met in a wine bar. Sue vaguely knew
Sheldon through a mutual friend. As they chatted, Sue's
voice grew progressively louder until she dominated the
conversation. She asked Sheldon what he liked in a
woman. He told her that he liked intelligent, interesting
women. When Sheldon asked what Sue liked in a man,
she shrieked with laughter and said, so that everyone
could hear, 'I like a man with a big firm tushy,' and
grabbed his bottom. Shocked and completely turned off
by her behaviour, Sheldon quickly made his excuses
and left.

The following day, Sue phoned Sheldon's friend. 'I
think I could have a long-term relationship with Sheldon,'
she said, having no idea that Sheldon would never ever
think of seeing her again. He described her as having an
aura of desperation.

Sue felt that she had to behave in a brash, aggressive
way to attract a man and continued to repeat this pattern
until she underwent therapy and took a self-esteem
course, through which she realised that such behaviour
was unacceptable.

Sue has now met Roger and is to marry him next year.
She admits that she would have remained on her own if
she had not altered her approach to men. She
acknowledges that she felt so unhappy and so full of self-
hatred that she did not realise how her behaviour had
appeared to men.

✴✴✴✴✴✴✴✴✴✴✴✴✴✴✴✴✴✴✴✴✴

In order to understand how Dragon Women have evolved, it
is necessary to examine the changing role of women over the
last few hundred years. Women have come under many

influences during this period. The traditional roles, demeanour and characteristics of western women, at least, have changed beyond all recognition. Women's new role in today's society is a distortion of the suffragette goals of emancipation and justice and we have become caricatures of the liberated woman that feminists once envisaged. Men don't like this new persona and, I suspect, neither do most women. The Dragon Woman personality has appeared only recently – born from women's fear of returning to the oppression they suffered in the past. There is no need to fear such a return unless women's own unreasonable behaviour generates a backlash. Germaine Greer states in *The Whole Woman*: 'If women can see no future beyond joining the masculinist élite on its own terms, our civilisation will become more destructive than ever. There has to be a better way.' I agree.

Women must soften and evolve into 'www.woman', who is warm, welcoming and wise, without being afraid that this means surrendering, returning to the past or giving in. The 'www.woman' of the new millennium knows that sensible compromise leads to happiness and can avoid any unnecessary conflict with her partner. She doesn't need to fight anymore because she has arrived.

# CHAPTER 2

# So What Planet Did Dragon Women Come From? Earth!

*Women as a class have never subjugated another group. We have never marched off to wars or conquest. We have never been involved in a decision to fight for foreign markets on distant shores. These are the games men play, not us. We want to be neither oppressors, nor oppressed. The women's revolution is the final revolution of them all.*

– Susan Brownmiller

Men didn't suddenly lean forward one morning over breakfast to find Dragon Women sitting there in place of their wives. Dragon Woman emerged gradually as a result of social and political changes over many hundreds of years.

There have always been strong individual women who have stood out in history: Boadicea, Cleopatra, Elizabeth I, Margaret Thatcher. From the beginning of documented history, there have been rumblings of feminist ideals and I feel sure that Eve expressed hers, but the only person available to listen was Adam, and of course she got him into trouble with God.

More recently however, in Europe in the 1600s, there were strong mutterings from women about rights they felt should be recognised, but it was not until women organised themselves on any meaningful scale that any real change began to happen.

In the mid-eighteenth century in Europe, when men challenged the feudal system, women in turn challenged the domestic tyranny forced upon them by men. Many women believed themselves to be slaves in the home and sought some means of breaking free.

> *England is the seat of the most abominable despotism,*
> *where laws and prejudices submit woman to the most*
> *revolting inequality. A woman may inherit only if she*
> *has no brothers, she has no civil or political rights and*
> *the law subjects her to her husband in every respect.*
> – Flora Tristan

In England in 1792, Mary Wolstonecraft wrote *A Vindication of the Rights of Women*, one of the foundation stones for the women's emancipation movement, of which Wolstonecraft was a founding member. She believed that women should have the right to work and be educated outside the home, and that civil and political rights should be granted to them. She wrote, 'I do earnestly wish to see the distinction of sex abolished altogether *save where love is concerned*'. There has been much debate about what she meant by this. Although Wolstonecraft believed that women were born equal and men taught them to be subordinate, I believe that she intended to say that women's loving relationship with men must be preserved at all costs, because this is the foundation of civilised society.

> *Men need women more than women need men, and*
> *so, aware of this fact, Man has sought to keep Woman*
> *dependent upon him economically as the only method*
> *open to him of making himself necessary to her.*
> – Elizabeth Gould-Davies

Subsequently, mid-nineteenth-century Britain's Industrial Revolution produced a surge of working women, mainly domestic servants, milliners, seamstresses, farm labourers and governesses. Whereas previously women had worked at home, on the farm, in craft or domestic industries, they now worked in groups in factories and had wages paid directly to them. Most women were still, however, excluded from the professions and formal education; the best hope for their futures lay in marriage. Married women began to perceive themselves as prisoners because, while they were single, they kept whatever income they had but, upon marriage, all their property and earnings were forfeited to their husbands.

In 1856, again in England, Barbara Leigh Bodichon and Bessie Rayner Parks organised a committee to collect petitions for a married women's property bill which would allow wives to keep their own property and income. But it wasn't until 1882 that this finally became law. It remains the precedent for today's divorce laws in the UK and elsewhere.

> *The whole moveable or personal estate of the wife, whether acquired before or during the marriage, shall, by operation of law, be vested in the wife as her separate estate and shall not be subject to the jus mariti (marriage law).*
>
> – Married Women's Property Act (1882)

Until the twentieth century with the arrival of Emmeline (Emily) Pankhurst, British feminists concentrated on the subordination of women to men, while some, like Josephine Butler, argued that women had a distinct culture of their own that was morally superior to men's. She said that women were purer, with little or no need for sex – unlike men, who she said were ruled by animal passions. Ironically, merely one hundred years later, feminists were to fervently argue for 'free love'. In 1903, Pankhurst shifted women's focus towards political action and founded the Women's Social and Political Union (WSPU) with her daughters.

> *The fundamental reason that women do not achieve*
> *so greatly as men do is that women have no wives.*
> – Professor Marjorie Nicholson

Determined to obtain for women the right to vote, this well-organised group was prepared to use any means to secure it. They chained themselves to railings, confronted politicians and went to great lengths to draw attention to their cause. In 1906, they were nicknamed 'suffragettes' by the *Daily Mail* newspaper, and thus began the fight which created the modern Dragon Woman persona which men fear and abhor.

To be fair, the suffragettes used peaceful methods for some years without success, but after being ignored by the men in power for what they felt was too long, in 1912 they resorted to violent means to get their attention – breaking street lights, setting fire to letter boxes, daubing seats on Hampstead Heath and bombing empty houses and unused railway stations. They even went so far as to break into the Jewel Room at the Tower of London. The most extreme action was taken by Emily Davison, who ran onto a race-course and was fatally injured by King George V's horse. The British public gradually grew disenchanted with them because of their increasingly dangerous stunts to gain attention, and the movement all but stopped in August, 1914, with the outbreak of the First World War. During the war, the WSPU was converted into recruiting women as workers for the home front and, in 1917, became known as the Women's Party.

By the end of the war, it was abundantly clear that women had made an enormous contribution to the war effort, working as nurses, bus drivers, factory hands and farm labourers, as well as continuing to carry out their domestic duties, while their men fought for king, country and liberty. Many were reluctant to give up their new-found economic independence when the men returned after the war. Women's roles had changed dramatically and for ever.

> *Men have power and a power complex; women just have a complex.*
>
> – Yvonne Roberts

In 1918, women over 30 were given the vote for the first time, but only if they were university graduates, householders, or wives, or paid a yearly rent of at least five pounds.

The issue of women's rights rose again after the Second World War when women sought recognition for their essential contribution to winning the war. Some continued to work as they had while men were away fighting.

However, the 1950s brought a backlash against working women. Unemployment rose, and men without jobs became resentful towards the women who had taken their places in the labour market. A public campaign urged women to return to their homes and look after their families.

> *Twenty million young women rose to their feet with the cry 'We will not be dictated to' and promptly became stenographers.*
>
> – G. K. Chesterton

Women's reaction to this propaganda from the media undoubtedly fuelled the explosion of feminism that occurred in the 1960s. As financial prosperity increased and women obtained greater access to education, in Britain and throughout the world, women now felt that they should be treated as equals in the workplace. They perceived that they continued to be trapped in a secondary role of looking after men, both at home and at work, so they began to campaign for equal pay, benefits and sexual autonomy through the Women's Liberation Movement, which fought against the oppression and subordination of women. Preaching the message that everyone should have freedom and the opportunity to express themselves, they began to attack taboos about sex (and the right of females to experience it as men always had), male structures and authority, managing to enforce claims made by women for salaries closer to those of men.

Changing social attitudes paved the way for the Abortion Act of 1967 and easier divorce with the Divorce Act of 1969. The introduction of oral contraceptives ('The Pill') offered protection against unwanted pregnancies and greater sexual freedom. Slogans such as 'Y be a wife?' appeared everywhere. Liberationists claimed that the ordinary nuclear family (consisting of a husband, wife and two children) was dysfunctional and that it oppressed women and produced neurotic individuals.

The strong feelings many women felt about what they perceived as social tyranny erupted in 1968 outside the Miss America Beauty Pageant in Chicago, where liberationists threw objects symbolic of women's oppression, such as girdles, dishcloths, false eyelashes and bras, into a 'Freedom Trashcan' – and thus was born the notion of the 'bra-burning women's libber', although, in fact, no one ever set light to them. Forever known thereafter as 'the bra-burning 60s', this flamboyant decade encouraged the idea that morality should come from within and be based on love. Unfortunately, this message was oversimplified by media propaganda so that the incidence of sex outside marriage increased and the divorce rate rose.

> *Much male fear of feminism is infantilism – longing*
> *to remain the mother's son, to possess a woman who*
> *exists purely for him. These infantile needs of adult*
> *men for women have been sentimentalised and*
> *romanticised long enough as love. It is time to*
> *recognise them as arrested development.*
>
> – Adrienne Rich

In the 1970s, there emerged three different types of feminism:

- social feminists opposed to male domination and class exploitation;
- liberal feminists who believed that equal rights should be given to women; and
- radical liberationists, who held women-only campaigns and demonstrations to build a women's culture against men's violence towards women, rape and pornography.

Female liberationist superstars already on the scene, like America's Gloria Steinem and Britain's Germaine Greer, were joined by others who had great impact. Books like *The Female Eunuch*, *Women's Consciousness*, *Man's World* and *Conditions of Illusion* were bestsellers, each of them preaching the same message of women's oppression.

> *Can you imagine a world without men? No crime and*
> *lots of happy fat women.*
>
> – Marion Smith

Then the Liberation Movement exploded into the Sisterhood. New young feminists impatient to 'immediately' have more freedom became overzealous and disrespectful, refusing to allow viewpoints other than their own to exist.

Thus, political correctness was born, which has gone from strength to strength, and is now strangling common sense.

> *The good part of being a feminist is about frightening men. Of course, there is a lot more to feminism, but scaring the shit out of the scumbags is an amusing and necessary part because, sadly, a good many men still respect nothing but strength.*
>
> – Julie Burchill

Political correctness has now had an impact on every area of modern life. Valuable ideas which would have continued to benefit all women are now dogma. This extremism initially arose from women's bitterness at failing to be properly recognised at work, in politics and in education, but has now imploded to destroy the basic and fundamental cornerstone of society – namely: relationships.

> *I am furious about the women's liberationists. They keep getting up on soapboxes and proclaiming that women are brighter than men are. That's true, but it should be kept very quiet or it ruins the whole racket.*
>
> – Anita Loos

Since the 1970s, women's working patterns have shifted from more part-time to full-time work outside the home. Better pay and a broader range of occupations are available to them, and this has affected the balance of power in male-female relationships.

> *Real equality is going to come, not when a female Einstein is recognised as quickly as a male Einstein but when a female schlemiel is promoted as quickly as a male schlemiel.*
>
> – Bella Abzug

Throughout the 1980s, the Women's Liberation Movement was critical of male domination, particularly regarding their position in the family and the limitations they saw that men imposed on women. This exploded into an attack by radicals on the traditional family and its values, which encouraged society to grant women choices about whether to get married, stay married or even reproduce.

> *To be a liberated woman is to renounce the desire of being a sex object or a baby girl. It is to acknowledge that the Cinderella–Prince Charming Story is a child's fairy tale.*
>
> – Claire Boothe-Luce

Then, in 1990s Britain, the way that equal pay and sex discrimination legislation was implemented caused many men to experience a new sense of injustice at the hands of women in the workplace. They perceived a dichotomy between women's wish to be treated as equals at work and legislation that, in favouring women, became unfair to men.

> *During the feminist revolution the battle lines were simple. It was easy to tell the enemy – he was the one with the penis. This is no longer strictly true. Some men are okay now. We are allowed to like them again. We have to keep them in line, of course, but we no longer have to shoot them on sight.*
>
> – Cynthia Heimel

A report published in Britain by the Head of the Equal Opportunities Commission Julie Mellor, in March, 2000, suggested that men are being positively discriminated against in the workplace because they do not have the same access to the Sex Discrimination Act as women. Men are saying that women who have behaved in an unacceptable manner in the workplace are using legislation to avoid dismissal and to lodge unfair claims.

> *Women who can, do. Those who cannot become*
> *feminists.*

– Anon

Many men believe that the liberation pendulum has swung too far in women's favour so that women now expect society to be constructed for their pleasure, work and political ends at the expense of men. Women seem to be blinkered to the effects this is having on the growth and development of men.

> *I disagree with the current phase of feminism.*
> *Women's sexual power is an enormous force.*
> *Feminists think only in terms of social power.*

– Camille Paglia

This shift in social attitudes is reflected in the media. As Dillon Jones, editor of the men's magazine *GQ*, observed in February, 2000, 'Gone are the days when characters such as Gene Hackman as Popeye Doyle in *The French Connection*, or Ted Danson's Sam Malone, give men something to live up to.' There are no more heroes like John Wayne. Jones goes on to say that on television women are portrayed as savvy, sassy girls about town and men as neurotic clowns and 'dehumanised expressions of the last remnants of viable manhood'. In advertisements, women are often seen as all-conquering modern consumers while men are no longer strong, silent breadwinners but vaguely comical saps.

> *Once a woman is made a man's equal, she becomes*
> *his superior.*

– Margaret Thatcher

What has evolved today, as these media images convey, is not women seeking equality, as the feminists proclaim, but superiority. Men today are so frightened of being politically incorrect, and of women's power, that they tend not to speak out about women's behaviour when they disapprove of it. They claim that women perceived that, in order to achieve equality, they had to prove not only that they were men's equals but that they were far better than men. Their resentment about having to do this has made them unfriendly and cold towards men, in the workplace and at home.

> *Feminism is the result of a few ignorant and literal-minded women letting the cat out of the bag about which is the superior sex. Once women made it public that they could do things better than men, they were of course forced to do them. Now women have to be elected into political office, get jobs as officers of major corporations and so on instead of ruling the earth by batting their eyelashes the way they used to.*
> – P. J. O'Rourke

Men say that they used to be able to laugh with their women colleagues about all kinds of issues, including femininity, but women have now become hostile at work. They no longer wish to be seen as 'one of the gang' and constantly fight for equality. They have become angry and stubborn in their views. Sexual discrimination ideas now have taken over the workplace with such extreme force that men are reluctant even to say 'Good morning' for fear that it will be misinterpreted as an unwelcome advance.

From friendly working conditions in which people could grow together, it seems that we have developed sterile, cold environments where people work in fear of each other instead of in harmony. Women at work have become progressively more arrogant and domineering. As long as they feel they cannot move through the glass ceiling of employment, women will continue to resent their male colleagues.

Dragon Woman now struggles with the Dragon King idea of the past, while men have changed, often without women even noticing. Women must now face the sad truth that the oppressed have become the oppressors. Men are claiming that they dare speak about this only to a therapist, a marriage-guidance counsellor – or a divorce lawyer.

> *It is probably true to say that the largest scope for change still relies on men's attitude to women and women's attitude to themselves.*
>
> – Vera Brittain

# CHAPTER 3

# The Dragon Drone

*Men seldom make passes at a girl who surpasses.*
– Franklyn D. James

As a working woman, wife and mother, I am aware of the dilemma that working women face. We are expected to be multi-functional – to work, to run a home, to be a wife and mother, to compete in the workplace, and to succeed in all these areas. In 1998, Nicola Horlick suggested that women can have it all: work, home life and happiness. However, as a divorce lawyer, I can say with absolute authority that this is only achievable when working women adopt a sensible approach to life. If they do not do so, their relationships suffer. Divorce statistics prove that this is so.

Many working women are finding that the combination of all of these roles is too much for them. Instead of recognising that this is the case, they are refusing to do so. It is quite clear that by slightly altering their perceptions and approach, they could cope perfectly well, but, instead of squarely facing the situation, many women are becoming aggressive, angry and resentful towards their partners – and creating bedlam. The reason this is happening is that women feel let down and insufficiently supported by their partners. Women's consequent anger has led to more relationship breakdowns than any other single factor in the last five years.

Many women balk at the suggestion that they are to blame for the breakdown of relationships, but the sad fact is that they are.

> *Do you know what it means to come home at night to*
> *a woman who will give you a little love, a little*
> *affection, a little tenderness? It means you are in the*
> *wrong house, that's what it means.*

> – Henry Youngman

**CASE STUDY** • • • • • • • • • • • • • • •

Audrey came to see me in a very distressed state. She could not understand why her husband had left her for a business colleague. She saw herself as totally blameless. She was stunned and confused when her husband served a divorce petition on her based upon her unreasonable behaviour. In the petition, her husband referred to her as always being angry, constantly shouting at him, particularly upon her return home from work. He said that she was domineering and aggressive and too needy. Her body language showed that she was always ready for a fight.

When Audrey and I took an honest look at the way she had behaved over the preceding two years, she realised that her husband was right. He had been trying to talk to her for months about how miserable he was, but she hadn't wanted to listen. She was so preoccupied with her own problems at work that she had shut him out.

• • • • • • • • • • • • • • • • • • • • • •

Considering the cases I have handled over the last few years and the specific complaints made by men involved in divorce proceedings about their wives' behaviour at home, it appears that men today divide working women into four categories:

# The Sergeant-Major Drone

The Sergeant-Major Drone is usually a high-flyer who wants to regiment everyone at home as she does at work. This category comprises politicians, barristers, solicitors, company directors and accountants. She believes that life should be run in a completely orderly way. The house must always be tidied to the highest possible standard and her husband must be impeccably turned out, as must their children. She sets standards so high that no one can possibly attain them. She treats her entire family as if they are children, particularly her husband. If he comes home late from work, she scolds him with, 'And where have *you* been?'

> *Other people are not in this world to live up to your expectations.*
>
> – Fritz Perls

This type of working woman tends to generate mutiny in the home. Statistics show that her children are more likely than those of other women to rebel or to leave home early. So, too, will her husband, unless his terror keeps him there. He is likely to escape round to friends' houses, the pub or the golf club on any pretext so as to avoid her criticisms. She is perfect, beyond reproach and never wrong. Armed with an inalienable faith in her own ability and opinions, she is organised, poised and unflappable, and her husband fantasises every day that she will get something wrong.

> *Give a woman a job and she grows balls.*
>
> – Jack Gelber

**CASE STUDY** ●●●●●●●●●●●●●●●

At work, everyone jumped to attention when Barbara barked an order. She ran a large department and could easily organise forty men and women. She had even reorganised other departments to increase productivity.

But there was one area which Barbara couldn't seem to organise, and that was her own home. Her daily house cleaner was reliable, her weekly deliveries were acceptable, and the dog and cat behaved perfectly well. However, try as she might, her husband Richard would not be house-trained. When she came home from work, she still had paperwork to do, and where was Richard? Taking a nap! Reading the newspaper! Or, worse still, wasting his time watching television. Barbara was forever fuming about him. Why wouldn't he do his allotted tasks, according to the rota she had pinned on the wall? The more Barbara stormed, the more Richard behaved like a naughty child.

Richard found Barbara's behaviour more and more overwhelming. She had turned from his wife into his mother. And boys rebel against their mothers. After twenty years, Richard had had enough and invoked his final rebellion: divorce.

* * * * * * * * * * * * * * * * * * * * * *

# The Hysterical Dragon Drone

The next category of Dragon Woman Drone, often described by husbands in divorce proceedings, is the Hysterical Drone. This is a woman who is totally disorganised, both at work and at home. She tends to take on more work than she can ever cope with, unable either to say no or to implement the changes necessary to make her life less stressful. She lives in a permanent crisis. Because her home is as chaotic as her job outside it, she always feels at a loss at home. She approaches every domestic problem hysterically, whether it is dealing with the Gas Board or a broken appliance, and she sees anything that disrupts her routine as deliberate sabotage by some unseen force working against her. She personalises every event and is constantly shouting at her family, blaming them for not helping her, whereas the fault lies with her own tiredness (which, of course, is the result of her own lack of organisation). She pours out a constant flow of complaints about her work problems to her husband, who cannot wait to get away.

**CASE STUDY** • • • • • • • • • • • • • •

When Sheldon came to see me about his divorce, he was totally bewildered by the change in his wife, Sarah. He explained that Sarah had been perfectly normal until she started to work, then, he said, she became an alien. He described how Sarah would start screeching at him as soon as she had taken off her coat when she came home from work.

'I suppose you're going to tell me how tired you are!' she would shout with regularity.

He would reply that he hadn't even said hello yet.

If he did acknowledge that he was tired, but that he didn't see it as a crime, she would become even angrier, telling him he didn't have any idea what tired was. She said that she knew, because she had to go to work, look after the children, do the shopping, do the cooking, clear up and – what did he do? A rubbish job and then he came home.

Sheldon said that he felt furious when Sarah launched into her tirades. He believed that he contributed a lot. He paid all the household bills, the mortgage, and the children's school fees, and felt that he helped at home. His wife's suggestion that he didn't do anything drove him wild. Frequently he would find himself just walking out of the house seeking solitude.

In the end, he could take it no longer and separated from Sarah.

It is easy to see what was happening in their household. Sarah was exhausted, but, unable to ask for help in a constructive manner, she became aggressive and undermined Sheldon's efforts. He felt that his contribution ensured that they had a home and the bills were paid, which made him someone worthy of praise, not constant derision.

• • • • • • • • • • • • • • • • • • • • • •

This story is a very familiar one – as a divorce lawyer, I hear it on a regular basis. Neither party was willing to give in. Neither was willing to recognise that each had good reason to be upset. If Sarah had asked sensibly for help and explained her unhappiness, or, better still, better managed household tasks, and Sheldon had done the same, their marriage would certainly have been saved.

## The Martyr Dragon Drone

This is the working woman who, in her quest to be universally liked, shoulders huge burdens, refusing any offers of help. She has grown up believing that this would win her love and affection. Because she has always done everything, everyone in her family expects her to continue to do so. She slaves away in smouldering anger, hating everybody and everything, snapping at her family without explanation. They put her behaviour down to hormonal problems or stress at work, leaving her feeling ignored and misunderstood.

> *The Housewife – no one knows what her life*
> *expectancy is, but I have a horror of leaving this*
> *world and not having anyone in the entire family*
> *knowing how to replace a toilet tissue spindle.*
>
> – Erma Bombech

The Martyr, instead of expressing herself calmly and coherently, gives way to sudden, unaccountable outbursts, such as throwing all of her husband's socks out of the bedroom window or smashing crockery. Her repressed anger will either turn inwards, making her physically ill, or outwards, so that she sits glumly sulking or pouting every evening, to her family's bewilderment.

**CASE STUDY** ● ● ● ● ● ● ● ● ● ● ● ● ● ●

Philip sought my advice about instigating divorce proceedings a few years ago. He described Sally's behaviour in detail. She had been a loving wife, he said, and seemed to have an intuitive grasp of what made him happy. What had first attracted him to her was her sense of humour. She had an ability to laugh at the absurd and a way of making life seem happy. That, he said, was before she started working.

About two years after Sally started her job, in recruitment, her personality changed. When she came home, she no longer seemed pleased to see him or their children. She was constantly in a bad mood or monosyllabic. Her sense of humour vanished, and she rarely spoke without snapping.

One day, Philip came home from work to find that Sally had vandalised all of the model cars that he had built. His pride and joy, they had been displayed in the lounge. When he asked her why she had done it, Sally told him she felt her life was being destroyed and wanted to do the same to his.

Philip and Sally did not have counselling. They stopped communicating altogether, and were divorced.

Sally felt that she was being put upon by everyone and everything around her. Instead of dealing with the situation sensibly and obtaining help to save her relationship, she exploded.

● ● ● ● ● ● ● ● ● ● ● ● ● ● ● ● ● ● ● ● ●

# The Dragon Persuader

Although, technically, no mere Dragon Drone, this kind of working woman, accomplished in the arts of subtlety and gentle persuasion, knows how to get her entire family to help her without a whimper. She achieves this by employing humour and stating preferences rather than making demands. She asks for help when she needs it, with feminine charm. Because her husband and children are happy to help her, she has time to sit down with them to chat and pursue her own activities. Blessed with a sense of humour and a happy, light attitude to life, she has transcended Dragonhood. She is a www.woman.

*I hate housework. You make the beds, you do the dishes and six months later you have to start all over again.*

– Joan Rivers

# CHAPTER 4

# How Dragon Drones De-Stress

*If you can keep your head when all about you are losing theirs, it's just possible that you haven't grasped the situation.*

— Jean Kerr

In order to get rid of stress, first you must know what it is and that you are suffering from it. Although many Dragon Drones may not realise or even have time to acknowledge it, they are suffering from stress. This is the cause of the aggressive, volatile behaviour men are complaining about in women. By applying stress-management techniques to help them, women can learn to cope with their many responsibilities.

Unfortunately, Dragon Women may be too arrogant to admit that they are under stress, and unwilling to reappraise their lives in order to minimise it, or to ask for help sensibly. Their refusal to take steps towards finding solutions to this problem means that they will continue to cause misery all about them. Put simply, they will be to blame for the breakdown of their relationships because they will take it out on men who will then leave them.

In an ideal world, if men were perfect and did Dragon Woman's bidding, she would not become so stressed, perhaps, but we don't live in such a world. Modern women have become so stressed that, even when men do help them, their aggression spirals out of control and harms their relationships.

# What Stress Is

So what is stress, and what can you do about it? Both men and women experience it. Positive stress allows you to deal with the task in hand, but, if you allow minor stresses to build up to the extent that they take over and stop you from functioning normally, you simply burn out.

Thousands of years ago, primitive man had what psychologists call a 'flight or fight response' to danger. He could either fight to repel aggressors, or run away from them. He would have an adrenaline rush, after which his body would then settle down. However, because modern life does not provide outlets for this surge in adrenaline levels, our bodies do not settle down, and leave us on a constant 'high'. This sort of stress invokes physical changes in our bodies: our heart and pulse rates go up, our muscles tense, we begin to sweat, and our blood pressure rises; in this state, women produce fewer female hormones, which causes even more tension. Heart attacks and strokes are among the diseases directly linked to negative forms of stress. In addition to these physical signs of stress, identifiable and repeated emotional symptoms are produced which affect every area of our lives. These include:

Anger
Anxiety/Fear
Depression
Fear of disease
Feelings of isolation and
 loneliness
Frustration
Impaired memory
Inability to cope and
 make decisions

Inability to relax
Inappropriate outbursts
 of rage
Irrationality
Irritation
Lack of interest in life
Lethargy
Loss of humour
Low self-esteem

It is clear that these symptoms are likely to cause problems and misunderstandings in relationships, particularly if both partners are experiencing similar ones. Everyone has stress in life. What we must do is learn to manage it.

Working women often find themselves in a cycle where they don't have breakfast, never exercise, fail to complete tasks and constantly rush to meet deadlines. Too tired to sleep when they go to bed, they oversleep and cannot get to work on time the next day. This can become a vicious downward spiral that produces stress, tension and the emotional symptoms listed above.

This syndrome places intolerable pressures on women's relationships with their partners and, ultimately, leads to irretrievable breakdown. However, if a couple can recognise that they are suffering from stress and actively apply themselves to undertaking a programme of healthy change, divorce can be avoided and their relationship saved.

> *If someone you marry changes so much in the last four years, i.e., to a veggie then a vegan and then a Buddhist and on top of that an animal rights activist and then a Green Party candidate, what can a husband do? (Divorce!)*
>
> – Extract from a district judge's law bulletin contained in the defence of a divorce petition

If you observe these signs in yourself and know that stress is affecting the peace of your household, you have two choices. You can allow the situation to worsen and see your relationship disappear, or you can take sensible active steps to halt its downward slide, and reap the benefits of a happy, stable relationship. It is your choice.

# How to Cope with Stress

If you are suffering from several items on the list on page 33, then you are suffering from stress and should introduce a process of slow, gradual change into your life so that you may turn it around.

## Find Ways to Enjoy Life

You could begin with what behavioural psychologist Derek Webster calls 'The Nurture Pie Method'. Now before you start to panic, in the mistaken belief that this adds cooking to your endless tasks of the day, calm down. This has nothing to do with cooking, baking or gathering ingredients. It is a simple, easy, helping process.

Take a piece of paper and draw a large circle in the middle. Inside the circle, write down all the things that make you feel good.

If you can't think of anything to write, you are suffering from burn-out. You are likely to be angry, aggressive and resentful. You may even become enraged by the thought of carrying out this experiment. If so, force yourself to remember the things that made you feel good before you became stressed.

If you still can't imagine anything, think of a sunny day, a glorious sunset, a bunch of beautiful flowers, music that you love, going to the cinema or reading an amusing book. Very soon, you will fill the circle. You will be surprised how many enjoyable things are no longer part of your life now that it has become dull, sterile and pressured.

The next step is to reintroduce all of these things back into your life, item by item. Don't set yourself unrealistically high expectations. If you try to cram in all of these activities at once, you may start to panic and see everything as yet another pressure. Instead, slowly build on the pleasures that these activities bring you, and you will start to put balance back into your life, and your negative feelings will fade.

As you gain self-confidence, you will be able to complete a 'nurture pie' with your partner. Put into it all the activities you both enjoy but have stopped doing. They will help to re-establish a happy relationship between you.

You will probably realise that you have stopped seeing, or even telephoning, your friends, because you felt you didn't have time to do so. The fun you used to have with them also should be injected back into your routine. Simply pick up the phone, ring one of them and arrange to meet. You have plenty of the time to do this if you organise yourself properly.

*A little of what you fancy does you good.*
— Marie Lloyd

The importance of having some time for yourself is borne out by a study carried out in February, 2000, by The Well-being Charity. This showed that if everything you do in life is for others, and you do nothing for yourself, it leads to stress, burn-out and resentment. Only one woman in three of those interviewed had any time for herself each day. Working mothers were the most stressed, with seven in ten reporting that they had no help at all at home. Well-being psychologist Sandy Mann states: 'Women are in danger of burn-out. It is a phenomenon of recent times. Women are making an impression in the workplace as well as handling their tradi-tional role of homemaker. Women need to try to take a little time out for themselves every day. Doing so could have a positive impact on their mental and physical health.'

The Well-being Charity launched a campaign called 'Dare to Indulge' on February 29, 2000, to persuade women to take a little time off for themselves. The date was significant. Being a leap year, it would add an extra 24 hours to the year, in which women could do something – just for themselves.

> *There is only one corner of the universe you can be*
> *certain of improving, and that is your own self.*
>
> – Aldous Huxley

## Reality and Irrationality

Psychologists have found that it is the way we perceive and interpret what happens to us, rather than the events themselves, that produces emotional distress. For the most part, we are the authors of our own tragedies. In many senses, we manufacture most of the dramas that we act out in life. Reality is rarely as awful, disastrous, terrible, disgusting, dreadful, humiliating or abhorrent as we believe it is or could be. Yet we tend to treat minor problems as though they were major catastrophes, often attaching undue negative significance to unimportant events. It is in our power to change the way we think and therefore to create more happiness in our lives. In fact, happiness usually arises from our ability to become absorbed in external activities rather than ourselves.

> *If you want to understand the meaning of happiness,*
> *you must see it as a reward, not as a goal.*
>
> – Antoine De Saint Exupery

Psychiatrist and psychologist Dr. Albert Ellis believed that most negative thinking stems from irrational beliefs. He found that irrational demands we make, upon both ourselves and others – demands which are impossible to meet – lead to stress. If you set standards for yourself that you or those around you cannot attain, you become frustrated, angry and irrational.

Below are irrational beliefs, identified by Dr. Ellis, commonly found in people who suffer from burn-out:

1. Everybody must love and approve of me.
2. I must be perfect in everything I do.
3. Some people are bad, wicked or awful and must be punished.
4. Things must go the way I want them to or everything is awful, terrible and disastrous.
5. Unhappiness is externally caused and I cannot control it unless I control the person causing it. I must be happy; you must make me happy; you must not make me unhappy.
6. I must remain upset or worried if faced with a dangerous or terrible reality.
7. It is easier to avoid responsibility and difficulties than to face them. I must not have to deal with problems; I must have an easy life.
8. I have a right to be dependent and people must be strong enough to take care of me.
9. My early childhood experiences must continue to control me and determine my emotions and behaviour.
10. Happiness can be achieved by inaction and endless leisure. I must not have to expend effort in order to become happy.
11. There is one precise and perfect solution and it would be terrible and catastrophic if this perfect solution were not found. I must find a perfect solution.
12. The world and other people must be fair and justice must triumph.

Irrational beliefs arise when we ignore reality and insist on having what we want. A Dragon Drone might say, for example: 'You must help me clear up this kitchen' or 'You ought to be helping'. The implication of these statements is that, unless you give me what I want, it will be awful and terrible and the world will be a terrible place. It would be more reasonable, and effective, if a woman expressed her desire as a preference (e.g., 'It would be nice if you helped me' or 'I would like it if you would help me').

So often in divorce proceedings, women claim that they can't get their husbands to help them. More appropriately phrased requests would work wonders for them, and vice versa.

Relationship psychotherapists demonstrate that using the right words enables us to achieve what we want. Avoiding using words like 'should, 'must', 'have to', etc., makes others more predisposed to being helpful. This technique has been successfully employed in many couple-therapy sessions.

Setting unrealistically high goals for those around you will make you angry, anxious, ashamed, guilty and depressed. But if you have a rational level of expectations of yourself and your family, you may express annoyance, concern, regret or sadness that your desires are not being met, but your behaviour will not be so dramatic or extreme. Remember, expressing a preference – such as 'I would prefer', 'I would like' or 'I would wish' – really does help.

It is important to remember that one unmet desire or mistake does not make you a failure. Neither does it mean, if you do something your partner doesn't like, that you are bad or wicked. It simply means that, like all of us humans, you are fallible. We all make mistakes.

> *There is the greatest practical benefit in making a few failures early in life.*
>
> – T. H. Huxley

I have found, particularly in divorce proceedings, that people who make sweeping generalisations tend to hold irrational, self-denigrating views. They may be one of four types:

1. The 'bad me'. They have a distorted view of their own value (for example, 'I am a wicked/bad person').

2. The 'less me'. They regard themselves as less worthy or less deserving than others as a result of their failure to live up to their own self-imposed demands.

3. The 'weak me'. They believe that they are weak, or weaker than others, because they don't live up to their self-imposed demands.

4. The 'poor me'. These are people who feel they do not deserve their fate, which they themselves have created.

> *I told my psychiatrist that everyone hates me. He said I was being ridiculous – everyone hadn't met me yet.*
>
> – Rodney Dangerfield

So many working women make irrational judgements when dealing with the responsibilities of home life. Simply re-evaluating or changing your way of looking at a situation will enable you to see that life is not so terrible and that problems need not bring a relationship to an end. A different approach can save it. Stress-management techniques may be utilised which will turn negative, irrational beliefs into positive ones.

> *A man who fears suffering is already suffering from what he fears.*
>
> – Michel de Montaigne

As Dr. Webster teaches in his stress management courses (based on the ideas of Dr. Ellis), it may help you to see more clearly what you may be doing to create unnecessary stress for yourself by considering your rational and irrational beliefs, eg.:

| Irrational belief | Rational belief |
|---|---|
| 1. *'It is absolutely necessary that everybody loves and approves of me.'* The truth is that it is impossible to please everyone in your life. | Even people who love you may occasionally be put off by some thing you do or say. This doesn't matter. You must lighten up and understand that you can't be loved by everyone. |
| 2. *'I must be perfect in everything I do.'* If you believe this, you will feel a failure when you cannot meet your unrealistic targets. Your low esteem will affect your relationship with your partner, and you will be afraid to attempt anything. | Nobody is all-perfect. Dragon Women want to be and become overbearing to all. It doesn't matter if a cup isn't put away once in a while. The world will not come to an end. No one will think any less of you if you aren't perfect – in fact, they will like you all the better for being fallible, like the rest of us. |
| 3. *'Some people are bad, awful or wicked and must be punished.'* While it is the case that some people might be, if you regard everyone around you as evil, you are being irrational. | If somebody has wronged you, it is preferable that they should change their behaviour rather than be punished. If you take the correct approach, you increase the chances that their behaviour will change for the better. If there is no realistic possibility of their being punished, you must divert your attention elsewhere. |
| 4. *'Things must go the way I want them to or they are horrible, awful and a disaster.'* The spoiled child or adult will meet any inconvenience, problem or failure to get their way by over-dramatising the situation. The result is intense irritation and stress. | These things happen to everyone, not just you. If your dishwasher breaks down, it isn't because the dishwasher devil has it in for you. He visits everyone from time to time. *Don't personalise – rationalise!* |

| Irrational belief | Rational belief |
|---|---|
| 5. '*Unhappiness is externally caused and I cannot control it unless I control other people.*' | You control your own emotions. Trying to control others will make you feel anxious and helpless. It cannot be done, so take charge of your life and create your own happiness. |
| 6. '*I must be prepared in case something disastrous happens, and work hard to avoid it.*' So many working women rehearse scenes of catastrophe, which increases their fear or anxiety unnecessarily and makes them unable to cope. | Save the fear response for actual or real danger. Don't anticipate disaster, or waste time and energy planning for unlikely scenarios such as: 'The repairman won't come, so I won't be able to cope, and I will get ill and everything will be terrible.' Lighten up. Think positively! The repairman *will* come. And if he doesn't, you will come up with another solution. |
| 7. '*It is easier to avoid responsibility and difficulties than to face them.*' So often we put off discussing important issues, particularly with our partners, like, 'I want another job', 'The roof has a hole in it', 'The car is making a peculiar sound' or 'We need to pay those bills'. As a result, the problems get worse and your worries about them build up into major stress. | If you deal with difficulties immediately, you will find that your problems recede. |
| 8. '*I need someone stronger or greater than I to rely on. Only someone like that can sort out things for me and help me.*' Assuming that someone else will always sort out your problems is a trap. If he or she ever doesn't or can't, you may fall apart. | You can sort out your own problems. If your partner can't help, bounce your idea or solution off a friend. It will make you feel much more confident about dealing with any future problems. |

*The optimist proclaims that we live in the best
of all possible worlds and the pessimist fears that
this is true.*

— James Cabell

**CASE STUDY** ✦✦✦✦✦✦✦✦✦✦✦✦✦✦

Marion and Gordon's daughter was about to get married.
Marion could foresee everything going wrong at the
wedding: the caterer not turning up, the flowers being
dead, the band not arriving, the groom not arriving, etc.
She worried about every single item, convinced
everything would go badly wrong. Gordon took a more
pragmatic approach. He was looking forward to his
daughter's wedding, even though he knew things might
not go according to plan. Everything he did to plan for the
great day was done with fun in mind. Marion spent the
whole of her daughter's wedding-day gloomy and
anxious, fretting about what might happen. She had a
miserable time. Gordon enjoyed every moment.

In therapy, when Gordon and Marion were trying to
sort out their marital problems, it emerged that Marion
took this negative approach to every event in their lives,
even everyday occurrences. Gordon couldn't cope with
Marion's irrational anticipation of disaster, and her
endless unnecessary agonising.

Eventually, Marion learned how to turn irrational
beliefs into rational ones. She is now far happier than she
has ever been.

✦✦✦✦✦✦✦✦✦✦✦✦✦✦✦✦✦✦✦✦

*Being popular is important; otherwise people might
not like you.*

— Mimi Pond

# Take Steps to Help Yourself

After you identify your irrational fears, consider what you can do to help yourself, and protect yourself from unnecessary stress.

## a. Switch Off

Many working women, when they come home from work, cannot switch off from worrying about their problems at work. According to a British Psychological Society report published in February, 2000, men find it hard to cope with their partner's work troubles on top of their own. The underlying reason for this is that men deal with their problems differently from women. They think through solutions quietly and tend not to talk them over at home. Women tend to talk and talk until they have exhausted the subject and their partners are at breaking-point. Women are also likely to discuss problems at ill-chosen times, such as the moment their partner walks in the door. They don't want a solution; they just want to talk about what is worrying them.

If you are one of these women, and your partner's ability to absorb your work problems is low, limit your discussion time with him and then phone a friend. Make it clear to your friend that you just want to talk through the problem and ask them to listen as you work out your options. Tell your partner that you value his opinion, but just want to sound out someone else about it. If you communicate your need to talk, he will then understand, and be relieved that he is not expected to keep listening. Operate the off button; he will love you for it. Talking about a problem endlessly does not necessarily solve it.

## b. Learn to Say No

Many working women say yes to everyone and then cannot cope with the number of tasks facing them. Learn to say no to some things that you don't want to do and can't possibly fit into your schedule.

## c. Stay Away from Negative People

If you are stressed and can give no more, do not surround yourself with people who are constantly leaning on you for advice. Psychologists have found that carers suffer from burn-out because they feel compelled to try to solve other people's problems. Take a step back and avoid other people's calls for a while. Give yourself time to recharge your batteries.

*He is a real pessimist – he could look at a doughnut and only see the hole in it.*

– Anon

## d. Realise Your Achievements

When you are stressed, you may see yourself in an irrational, negative light, blaming yourself for failing and being unable to cope. Tell yourself how well you have done and start to look at the things you can do, and you will find that you really are Superwoman.

*A pessimist is a man who is never happy unless he is miserable; even then, he is not pleased.*

– Anon

## e. Delegate

Working women often have the irrational belief that they can – and should – do everything themselves. When they can't, they fall victim to stress. Accept that you're not perfect and that you must delegate, then prioritise and organise your life sensibly. Don't be frightened to ask for help when you need it. Your colleagues and family will respect you more if you enlist their support rather than becoming angry or tearful and collapsing under the strain.

*Don't take life too seriously – you'll never get out of it alive.*

– Elbert Hubbard

# What to Do to Alleviate Stress

There are specific things you can do to alleviate and even eliminate stress.

## Try Alternative/Complementary Therapies

Relaxation is essential for de-stressing your life and avoiding arguments. You can relax in a number of different ways, a few of which are listed below to show you how to alleviate your misery and move beyond Dragon Woman states.

### a. Relaxation Tapes

If you do not have time to fit therapy classes into your timetable, then you can begin by listening to relaxation tapes. Many people employ visualisation techniques combined with positive thinking, e.g., you may be asked to close your eyes and think of a peaceful place – a sun-drenched beach or a clearing beside a woodland stream. This can help you to imagine positive outcomes for your problems, and distance you from those that surround you in your everyday life. Some tapes teach simple meditation techniques intended to induce a calmer state. One career woman I know listens to relaxation tapes on her way home from work on her car stereo. By the time she arrives at her front door, she has begun to unwind and feels better able to cope with stresses she must meet at home.

CAUTION: When you are driving, never listen to tapes that make you sleepy.

## b. T'ai Chi

This method for harmonising mind and body through slow, controlled movements comes from the Chinese Taoist system based on balancing Yin (cool, dark, negative energy) and Yang (hot, light, positive energy). Those who undertake this ancient form of meditation have found that it decreases depression, tension, anger, fatigue, confusion and anxiety.

## c. Pilates

Devised by Joseph Pilates in the 1920s to help dancers recuperate from injuries, this exercise system incorporates floor-based stretching exercises and breathing techniques to improve posture, realign the body and dissipate stress.

## d. The Alexander Technique

Developed by Frederick Alexander a hundred years ago, its aim is to improve the way we negotiate everyday movements like walking, sitting and lifting. The idea is to regain the natural, relaxed poise of children, eliminate physical symptoms of stress, improve posture and encourage better breathing.

## e. Yoga and Meditation

Many individuals find various forms of Yoga and Meditation a good way to release tension. These are essentially spiritual disciplines and so are not meant for relaxation only; however, hatha yoga teachers from the British Wheel of Yoga, for example, offer good, basic relaxation techniques.

### f. Massage

Massage can be an enormously beneficial way of ridding yourself of nervous energy and tension. Various kinds are available, including:

- Aromatherapy Massage (incorporates essential oils, some of which are most beneficial for de-stressing the body)
- Shiatsu (focuses on pressure points on the body to release tension)
- Reflexology (a form of foot massage which has been found to be useful for easing digestive problems and cramps, among other things)

## Improve Your Diet

Dieticians constantly remind us to pay attention to our body signals. We may notice that certain foods give us indigestion or headaches, but we go on eating them. Although we know that other foods help us to feel well and energised, we tell ourselves we don't have time to prepare them. Eating the wrong foods throughout the day makes us tired and irritable, and we invariably take this out on our partner or family. This is why eating a balanced diet can help to save a failing relationship.

> *Jack Sprat could eat no fat, his wife could eat no lean – a real sweet pair of neurotics.*
>
> – Jack Starky

It is a good idea to avoid sugary and high fat foods, and the following should be eaten on a daily basis:

- Fruits and Vegetables
- Carbohydrates/Starches
- Proteins
- Dairy Foods and Fats
- Vitamins and Minerals

The B vitamins, Calcium, Iron and vitamin E are particularly good for women to include in their diets, but it is advisable to consult a good book on nutrition for more detailed information.

Make the following part of your daily dietary regime:

- Always eat breakfast. If you miss breakfast, you will establish a pattern of tiredness before you have even begun your day. Eat porridge, for example, a carbohydrate which will release energy slowly all day. Certain starches, such as white bread, can make you feel sleepy.
- Never miss lunch. If you don't eat a proper lunch, you may be tempted to eat junk food in the afternoon, which will make you irritable, angry and tired by the end of the day.
- Try not to eat too late in the evening. If you eat early on, you will find it easier to sleep, you will not build up fats and put on weight so quickly, and you will wake up with more energy.

## Exercise

If you are exhausted and overburdened, the thought of exercise may make you want to scream. In your current state of mind, you may be unable to see that exercise is energising. When you exercise, oxygen-rich blood flows into the brain, releasing endorphins and making you feel better. Exercise energises your body and relaxes your mind at the same time.

> *I like long walks, especially when they are taken by people who annoy me.*
>
> – Fred Allen

Regular exercise reduces anxiety as effectively as meditation and other relaxation techniques. The benefits have been found to be long term, especially for those suffering from chronic anxiety. The longer you continue to exercise, the greater the effect it will have on you and the people around you, including your partner.

Exercise has also been found to enhance self-esteem, improve stamina and physical appearance, and combat depression.

> *The only reason I would take up jogging is so that I could hear heavy breathing again.*
>
> — Erma Bombeck

In addition, there is known to be a direct correlation between physical exercise and mental activity. Exercising improves our reaction time and our ability to solve problems. So, if you have a difficult problem at work to be solved, try exercising; it may well help you to think more creatively.

The National Institute of Health recommends thirty minutes of moderate exercise a day, which can be divided into three ten-minute bouts. If you have not exercised for some time, I would suggest that you start by walking and then go on – to cycling, swimming, tennis or other sports activities, dancing energetically, doing intense housework such as hoovering or dusting, and walking up and down stairs. You can progress by adding extra exercise sessions lasting twenty minutes each, three times a week.

Continually making excuses to avoid taking exercise may be indicative of a stress pattern. Stop making excuses and face the fact that exercise will help you. Think about joining a health club if you can afford it. There is no point in joining unless you go regularly, however. Exercise is an important part of your recovery plan, and doing as much exercise as you can comfortably fit into your routine will benefit both you and your family.

## Sleep

Many of my women clients complain that they are not sleeping properly. Transient insomnia goes away after a few nights, but short-term insomnia, which may last for two or three weeks, can be due to stress; it often stops when the underlying problem is solved. Chronic insomnia lasts more than a month and requires medical treatment. It may be caused by a psychological problem, but sometimes people get so used to not sleeping that they have to be retrained in order to sleep properly.

If the reason for your lack of sleep is something you can control, you must take steps to do so. Lack of sleep leads to anxiety, stress and a wide range of emotional problems.

> *Life is something you do when you can't get to sleep.*
> – Fran Lebowitz

Examining your behaviour patterns may suggest a solution. Sleep therapists recommend the following:

- Avoid nicotine. Sleep therapists suggest that you don't smoke, especially four hours before bedtime.
- Avoid alcohol, especially four hours or less before bedtime. Like caffeine and nicotine, alcohol acts as a stimulant and will not aid sleep.
- Don't eat a large meal late in the evening. A light snack of carbohydrates such as crackers, toast, cereal or bananas will help, but avoid sugary or salty foods, which can act as stimulants.
- Don't work, read, watch television or do anything in bed except sleep or make love. (This may be too difficult for most of us to manage, but at least try not to take your work to bed, because you will be unable to switch off and relax.)

- Establish a relaxed bedtime routine that will signal to your body and brain that it is time to sleep. Going to bed and getting up at the same time every day will help your body to establish a pattern.
- If you can't get to sleep after approximately thirty minutes, get up again and either do something relaxing or something that makes you sleepy.
- Your insomnia may be directly connected with aspects of your sleeping conditions. For example, your bed may be uncomfortable, too hard or too soft, the room may be too hot or too cold, the covers too heavy or too light, the pillows too soft or too hard. Take steps to make the necessary improvements.

## Take Stress Management Courses

If you believe that you are suffering from excessive stress or burn-out, and the self-help suggestions in this chapter are not enough to overcome the overwhelming difficulties you face, you may need a structured course to put you on the route to change. Medically supervised and approved courses can enable you to identify and deal with sources of stress. Some courses are conducted on a one-to-one basis and others in groups. They may be held at a clinic, or even require in-patient attendance.

> *Asking for help doesn't mean that you are weak or incompetent. It usually indicates an advanced level of honesty and intelligence.*
>
> – Anne Wilson-Scherfe

Be a www.woman and get help to deal with stress. You will thereby promote a happier environment for you and your family by banishing Dragon Woman from it altogether.

# CHAPTER 5

# Dragon Bullies at Home

*I am a marvellous housekeeper. Every time I leave a man, I keep his home.*

— Zsa Zsa Gabor

U nfortunately, stress isn't exclusive to the workplace or to women who work outside the home. It can also affect the partner who does not go out to work and stays home. Although it does so in a different way, the self-help techniques outlined in the last chapter for working women are equally relevant for her (or him!).

If you find yourself unable to cope, it is *you* who must take steps to alter your life. If you do not, your behaviour will affect your relationship badly.

The numerous cases of divorce and cohabitation in which I have been involved, including those referred to me by therapists and marriage guidance counsellors, indicate that Dragon Women at home tend to fall into these categories:

- The Nagger
- The Dominator
- The Perfectionist
- The Shopaholic
- The Silent Martyr
- The Sports Addict

*Women have many faults, men have only two: everything they say and everything they do.*

— Anon

# The Nagger

If there is one name that women particularly hate to be
called, it is a nagger. If there is one thing all men hate above
all, it is a woman who nags.

> *Nagging is failing to be there when a man wants her.*
> *It is a woman's greatest sin – except to be there when*
> *he doesn't want her.*

> – Helen Rowland

Women say they nag because men don't do what they ask.
Men say women just nag.

What is actually happening here is a conflict between
men's and women's different emotional and psychological
make-up. If by now you haven't realised it, men and women
*are* different! Men are solution-based, and get straight to the
point, whereas women tend to talk round in circles, endlessly going over a problem until they feel emotionally
satisfied. Men tend to see this as nagging.

In divorce proceedings, women often allege that when
they talked to their husbands about their feelings or worries,
they would not listen. This is because men feel that women
never get to the point. When appealed to, a man will feel
responsible for finding a straightforward solution to his wife's
problem, and will become impatient if this process cannot be
dealt with quickly.

Men generally want to know what is behind a conversation and what it is leading to. Frequently an exchange that
starts out about a broken light-bulb turns into a reproach
about how he hasn't kissed her hello. Men dread and avoid
emotional conversations, whereas women can talk about
feelings for hours. Men prefer a structured conversation with
a purpose, a short discussion and a solution. If you bring up
a string of topics, a man will shut off and resist conversing.

He will become angry, argumentative and refuse to talk. Worst of all, he will not take you seriously.

Women tend to build up lists of grievances and air them at the most inappropriate times. One of the most frequent complaints I hear in divorce proceedings concerns what I call 'The Doorstep Syndrome'. This is where men cannot even get over the doorstep before their wives bombard them with their problems. Husbands complain that their wives launch into a litany of criticisms before they have even taken off their coats, accusing them of earning too little, failing to help around the house and being bad fathers and unsupportive husbands.

**CASE STUDY** ● ● ● ● ● ● ● ● ● ● ● ● ● ● ●

Stephen had a particularly harrowing day at work and was really looking forward to coming home and unwinding with Patricia and their children. Before he even got through the door, Patricia greeted him with a look of disdain.

'The washing machine has broken down,' she snapped at him. 'The oven's cut out, so don't expect me to cook, and *your* children have been foul! As if that isn't enough, Samantha's leaving John! I can't take any more. It's so awful, I just want to die.'

Stephen told me that it was much the same every day. It made him want to turn around, get back into his car and drive back to the office, which seemed tranquil in comparison.

The next day he went to his office, where his easygoing and attractive secretary greeted him with a cup of coffee and an understanding 'How are you today?' Drawn to her, he started an affair. Stephen and Patricia were divorced.

There had been a gradual build-up of unnecessary stress in the home, for which Patricia was not wholly to blame, but she was constantly angry and had got into the habit of nagging Stephen remorselessly. She kept telling

> him that everything was falling apart at home, as if it was
> his fault. She 'awfulised' every minor incident.
> Overwhelmed by the barrage of her emotions, Stephen
> shut himself off from her.

• • • • • • • • • • • • • • • • • • • • • •

Men want to unwind at the end of the day, read the newspaper, eat and watch television before their partners offload their problems. Our brains have been found to be physiologically different and men process and deal with information differently from women. They cannot recover from the events of the day, for instance, and cope with an emotional onslaught at the same time. Their brains simply can't take the strain.

I am not suggesting that Patricia shouldn't have told Stephen about her problems, because bottling them up would be equally stressful, but that she should have given him a chance to relax first. She should have calmly told him, 'I had some problems with machines today that I need to talk to you about. Not now, but when we have both unwound. It won't take long, and I'm sure you'll come up with a good solution.' Allocating a time and a goal for the discussion will ensure he gives it his full attention.

When men feel they are being criticised by a woman, they become uncooperative and hostile. They will change the subject and/or verbally attack her. The reason is that women often veer away from the issue under discussion, saying things like: 'And you don't really love me or care about me – I know, I can feel it!' This kind of throw-away, apparently irrelevant comment infuriates men. 'What does the washing machine breaking down have to do with me loving you?' they will exclaim, exasperated. If your partner fails to respond to your initial problem (because he is tired or can't cope with you going on and on about it) and switches off, you may subjectively interpret this to mean that he is not listening and doesn't care. Once you realise that your own irrational belief is causing a problem, it won't be a problem any more.

**CASE STUDY** ● ● ● ● ● ● ● ● ● ● ● ● ● ● ●

Suzanne and Gary had been married for seven years. They had two children whom Suzanne looked after, and Gary went out to work.

After about six years, a pattern started to develop. Every time Gary came home from work, Suzanne would pounce on him with all kinds of dilemmas and dramas. He would tell her that he was tired and that he would like to eat first and then they could sort out whatever the problem was.

Suzanne would sulk throughout dinner and then, like clockwork, tell him, 'I want to talk about us.'

Gary would respond with, 'Maybe you should see your mother more. I'm going to watch television.' Inevitably Suzanne would then fly into a rage.

I suggested that he and Suzanne go to marriage-guidance counselling, as Gary really didn't want the marriage to end but simply couldn't cope with her behaviour any longer. Counselling enabled Gary to express how he felt.

He said that conversations like those Suzanne instigated every day made him anxious. She always made him feel that it was his fault that things were going wrong. When she threw everything at him at once, he just couldn't take it all in. All the emotional stuff she brought up made him feel pressured and confused, so that he lost his temper and usually walked out.

Gary and Suzanne were able to resolve their problems, because Gary learnt to express his frustration and admit that he found it difficult to talk about emotion, and Suzanne realised that men react in this manner; it wasn't just Gary. The therapist got them to focus on things they could do as a couple, rather than as individuals at war with each other. Gary and Suzanne are still happily married.

● ● ● ● ● ● ● ● ● ● ● ● ● ● ● ● ● ● ● ● ●

In many divorce cases, men complain that their wives bring up problems, often of an emotional nature, just before they go to bed. This is as infuriating to men as raising them when they have just come home from work. The husband will usually ask if they can talk about it in the morning, but his wife will not be put off.

In many couples-therapy sessions, it has emerged that the man's response to being asked to deal with emotions late at night is one of anger, as he feels it is the wrong time to bring up such issues. Afraid that his partner is likely to keep talking *ad infinitum*, and that he will never get any rest, the man tends to be unresponsive, just saying 'Yeah' or 'Right' occasionally, and then to fall asleep. This leaves the woman feeling even more frustrated.

It is important to understand that men don't want to have these late-night conversations. They are too tired to talk and don't like feeling that they are not in control of such a situation.

> *Never go to bed mad. Stay up and fight.*
> — Phyllis Diller

When men describe women 'nagging', they are usually referring to their tendency to think aloud, and to what I call 'dog and boning'. This is the feminine trait of not allowing a criticism or row to finish but to keep returning to it again and again, even when a man has apologised and a solution has been found.

Many husbands involved in divorce proceedings complain that if they apologise, their wives then want to know why. It is at this point that Colditz Man puts on his coat and looks for his car keys. Some psychologists describe this as women's slower way of signing off from an argument. Men describe it as nagging.

*A loving wife will do anything for her husband except stop criticising and trying to improve him.*

— J. B. Priestley

## The Dominator

The Dragon Dominator (the same character as the Dragon Bully in Chapter 1) wants to be in control of everything and everyone. Usually her mother was dominant in her family and, in her search for a husband, she gravitated towards a man who has either had a dominant mother himself or whom she believes is easy to control.

*Women would rather be right than reasonable.*

— Ogden Nash

She decides everything that happens in their relationship. She makes all their social arrangements, plans their holidays and books the restaurants when they go out. She is the one who walks into the restaurant first, gives the name of the reservation, asks for the bill, orders the wine and tells her husband what to order. She tells him how he is feeling, what he should do, what he should wear, whom he should telephone and how he should run his career. She decides when they should move home or redecorate; she does the hiring and firing and talks for both of them.

*A man finds himself by finding his place and he finds his place by finding appropriate others that need his care and that he needs to care for. Through caring and being cared for a man experiences himself as part of nature. We are closest to a person or an idea when we help it grow.*

— Milton Meyeroff

The Dominator often feels that she is ensuring that the relationship lasts by managing everything in it, but what she is actually doing is strangling it, emasculating and frustrating her partner in the process. To understand how her partner is feeling, she should remember that, since the beginning of time, men's role has been that of the provider. Primitive men hunted for food while their women were gatherers who also tended the home and cared for the children. A man naturally wants to protect and provide. When a woman usurps these functions, he feels unhappy and angry. We are all constantly changing and developing. The Dominator stunts her partner's growth by doing the growing for both of them, and undermines his self-esteem.

**CASE STUDY** ● ● ● ● ● ● ● ● ● ● ● ● ●

Georgina met and married Neil when they were nineteen. Neil's mother was very domineering and his father was a 'yes man'.

They soon drifted into a pattern where Georgina did everything. She would choose where they went out to eat and always insisted that she drove, particularly if they were accompanied by friends. She would order the wine for everyone without consulting them, and order Neil's food before he even opened his mouth. On the one occasion when Neil said he would prefer fish, she told him he wouldn't like it. She would light cigarettes and pass them to him even if he didn't want them, and would always be the one to ask for the bill, which she would then check and pass to Neil for payment. In restaurants, Georgina frequently complained that it was too hot or too cold, too empty or too full, too noisy or too quiet. She seemed to want to control the elements as well as everything else. She even took charge of Neil's working life, telling him to change jobs.

One day Georgina came home and found a note from Neil. It said: 'I am grateful for all you have done for me but I only have one life and I think I have the right to live it myself.'

> Georgina was shattered. She felt that she had borne all
> the responsibility in their married life. The fact was that she
> had overdone it. Colditz Man had made his escape, leaving
> no clues.

• • • • • • • • • • • • • • • • • • • • • • •

Why do Dominators behave this way? Psychologists tell us that often women like this had to prove themselves as children and cannot switch off as adults. If your mother constantly did everything for your father, you will probably repeat the pattern. Many Dominators are space invaders. Sometimes such women have an unspoken fear that, unless they carry all the emotional and physical burdens of the relationship, it will fail.

As we have seen, men and women approach problems very differently. Men tend to become quiet and withdrawn when they are mulling over things. Their partners should respect their needs and give them space, knowing that they will be ready to talk again as soon as a problem has been resolved.

In many divorce cases, the husband complains that if he becomes withdrawn, his wife, misunderstanding his need for some quiet time alone, will immediately assume she has done something wrong. She will ask him what the problem is, and whether he still loves her. This is not what he wants to hear; he simply needs space to work through whatever is bothering him.

Wives in the throes of divorce often complain that their husbands keep slamming out of the house. Their husbands comment that this is the only way they can get some space.

In a recent case of mine, a man complained to me that every time he cleaned his car, his wife would follow him and start helping him. This made him feel trapped and angry and it always led to arguments. She didn't understand that, while he was cleaning his car, he would think about any difficult problems he had and how to solve them. Had he communicated his needs and had she learned to give him space, they might still be married.

> *My husband said that he needed more space, so I locked him outside.*
>
>             – Roseanne Barr

Psychologist Barbara de Angelis describes these women as closing a vacuum. Women who walk into a room where no one is talking may feel compelled to start a conversation or to fill up drawers if they are empty. If they walk into a bachelor apartment which is sparsely decorated, they are urged to fill it up with cushions and bric-a-brac.

Georgina carried to excess this female tendency to fill silences with words, and time with activities. If she had allowed Neil to make at least some of the decisions in their lives, he would have felt more fulfilled as a man.

If you are a 'Georgina', recognise what you are doing and try to change your behaviour before it is too late. Remember to communicate your discovery to your partner, however, or else he will be baffled by the sudden transformation in you. If he realises that you are behaving differently for the good of your relationship, he will be ecstatic.

**CASE STUDY** ● ● ● ● ● ● ● ● ● ● ● ● ● ● ●

David was married to June for twenty years.

June was a Dominator. She would bully David and their children mercilessly, barking complaints at them. Like naughty children, they would all huddle in the lounge and giggle at her irrational behaviour. Not content with bullying her family, June particularly enjoyed bullying shop assistants. She was resentful of the fact that most of her friends worked, and felt undervalued. Instead of applying for a job, she allowed her frustration to smoulder. She would try to belittle anyone she met, reporting staff in shops if they did not serve her quickly enough, and calling them inefficient and stupid. She took forever to choose a simple item and then, without justification, would say, 'I don't like your mood,' and simply walk out. Anyone who came to her house to repair domestic appliances would receive the same treatment. Inspiring terror in others made June feel in control.

The final straw came when she decided to give away David's prize bike to the dustman. 'It's just cluttering up the place,' she said, chastising him like a petulant child. Finally David had had enough. He left home.

June was thoroughly puzzled. 'He'll be back,' she told her family. 'He's too reliant on me to manage by himself.'

After six months, David still hadn't come back and June began to realise that she couldn't always be in charge. Her irrational approach to life had come home to roost.

She contacted David and asked if they could go for therapy together. It was the first time he could remember her ever asking for anything. He agreed to her request. In therapy, after David explained how he and the rest of the family felt, June finally acknowledged how aggressively she had been behaving.

David and June have recently celebrated their twenty-fifth wedding anniversary. This time she asked *him* where he wanted the celebrations to take place.

* * * * * * * * * * * * * * * * * * * * * *

*A wise woman puts a grain of sugar into everything she says to a man and takes a grain of salt with anything he says to her.*

– Helen Roland

Most working women and women at home have come to realise that if they want help from their partners or to live in harmony, they have to approach matters in a rational way. Using the words 'Can you help me', 'I would like you to help me' or 'I need your help' will often unlock their partners' hearts and ability to assist them in everything they want.

Men don't like aggressive women. They like women to approach matters in a gentler way. Dragon Bullies and naggers often find themselves alone and unhappy. The www.woman knows that she must rid her life of irrational beliefs by taking a rational approach to matters at home.

> *If there is something you need to say to your loved one, remember to say it lovingly, as if holding his heart in your hands.*

> – Ellen Sue Stern

## The Perfectionist

Some women set unreasonably high standards at home which are unbearable for everyone. They are perfectionists.

**CASE STUDY** ● ● ● ● ● ● ● ● ● ● ● ● ● ● ● ●

Ronald's wife, Jane, was a perfectionist. Her hair and appearance were always perfect. She had been 'the perfect child', and had excelled at school, so her home had to be perfect too. She spent hours plumping up the cushions in the TV room and lounge. The towels in the airing cupboard were stored in ruler-straight piles and colour-coded. Socks, tee-shirts and underwear were always colour-coded, too. All their shoes were stored in labelled plastic bags.

Ronald was not perfect. He had been brought up in a relaxed home where everyone had 'mucked in'. His mother had worked, so the house wasn't always tidy, but no one minded.

After their children were born, Jane gave up work to look after them at home. Then the problems got out of hand. The family were not allowed to make a mess or even leave an unwashed glass or cup on a table. If Ronald put his feet up on the sofa, Jane would insist that he put them down, and would plump and replump the cushions throughout the evening.

As the children grew older, they became more resentful of Jane's behaviour. None of their friends wanted to come to their home after school because it felt so stiff and uncomfortable. Eventually, neither did Ronald.

One day he simply didn't come home. He instructed a lawyer to write a letter saying: 'My client believes that you will find the home a lot tidier without him!' She then realised, too late, that her irrational standards had forced Ronald to plot his escape in true Colditz Man style.

● ● ● ● ● ● ● ● ● ● ● ● ● ● ● ● ● ● ● ● ● ●

Jane is now in a new relationship. Through therapy, she has learnt the following:

- There just isn't time to be perfect at everything; if I try to be perfect at one thing, I'm going to take time away from something else.

- Everyone's different, and no one can be expected to do everything perfectly.

- Even if I have the ability and the time to do a task, I still won't achieve absolute perfection; there will always be room for improvement.

- If I always expect perfection, I'll be continually frustrated, and I'll never give myself credit for what I achieve.

- If I demand perfection, I will be afraid of falling short of my target, and may end up doing nothing at all rather than risk failure.

- People who admit they aren't perfect are non-threatening to others; they can get along with them quite well and have satisfactory relationships.

- Just because someone does something better than me, it doesn't mean that they are a better person.

- I can't always expect to do things even as well as I have done in the past, let alone better. I may be distracted by other things, or feeling tired or ill. It is irrational to expect to function perfectly all the time.

# The Shopaholic

There are two kinds of shopaholic: social shoppers and bored shoppers.

## 1. Social Shoppers

Social shoppers are usually housewives. They may spend a whole day at a shopping centre with a friend, chatting for hours on end. Sometimes they lose sight of the family finances, and they may overspend simply to keep up with their friends. Husbands married to such women often complain that their wives lose all sense of time, and often come home just before they do. The social shopper may seem resentful that she is then expected to make a meal for her partner, or do any housework.

Over the last five years there has been a steady increase in the number of social shoppers in Britain, leading to a growing sense of resentment among the men whose needs are being ignored.

**CASE STUDY** ● ● ● ● ● ● ● ● ● ● ● ● ● ● ●

Denise loved to shop with her friend Lucy. They went out three or four times a week to the local shopping centre. They would put the children in the crêche and spend hours drinking coffee and trying on clothes.

Denise's husband, Larry, was aiming for promotion. He came home at about seven o'clock, bringing work with him. He could only spare about an hour to have supper and be with their children before he had to get back to work.

Week after week, Larry would come home to find Denise talking to Lucy on the telephone, having only just returned from a day out together. Denise had an au pair who did the housework, so, as far as Larry could see, it wasn't too much to expect for her to prepare their supper. Most days, however, she would tell him to get it himself.

Eventually Larry had had enough. He started an affair

at work and left Denise shortly afterwards.

Denise couldn't see Larry's problem. She said he was married to his work.

Unfortunately, because he was providing for the family, Larry felt justified in putting all his efforts into his work. Denise, on the other hand, put all her efforts into shopping, he said.

* * * * * * * * * * * * * * * * * * * * * *

Retail therapy is all very well, but it may push your partner into psychotherapy, or both of you into the divorce courts.

## 2. The Bored Shopper

Women who have money but nothing to do, or who are wives of wealthy husbands, shop because they get bored. These are the women who lunch and feel no compunction about spending what for most would be a week's wages on a handbag. These women are unhappy, frustrated and unfulfilled. Their only form of expression is to outdress their contemporaries. Often the cost of their shopping spirals completely out of control, and it is at this point that their husbands cut the purse-strings. Their wives' fury is then unleashed and a divorce lawyer is usually consulted.

If you are a bored shopper and find that even shopping is becoming boring, then you must take stock. There is more to life than this. Boredom may lead to stress and illness, and it is vital to find a focus for your life. Start a job, a hobby or do some voluntary work – then you can shop for fun.

# The Silent Martyr

In the last chapter, we met the martyr who works. The Martyr who doesn't work may feel she is making even more sacrifices than the salaried martyr.

Because of the example set for them by their parents, Silent Martyrs sacrifice their own needs and feelings for those of their partners, behaving to please them and always deferring to their wishes. Children who are strictly brought up tend to try to please others even in later life, which can build up bitter resentments. Many women feel that, in order to gain approval and love, they must subordinate their own desires and wishes to others.

So often in divorce cases, women tell me that they feel terribly isolated, having given up friends their partners didn't get on with or stopped seeing close family members. Sometimes, of course, it is men who make these sacrifices, but more often it is women who give up supportive relationships. It is often a case of 'divide and rule'. If people are cut off from friends and family, they are more easily controlled. They tend to give up their careers, hobbies, enjoyment of art, music, etc., to try to please their partners.

**CASE STUDY** ● ● ● ● ● ● ● ● ● ● ● ● ● ● ●

Elsa described herself as 'empty'. She said she didn't know who she was any more. She had become a robotic image of what she believed John wanted. She said she resented John for making her feel 'like an amoeba'. She hated herself, but she hated him more. Elsa told me she was always moody and sulky when John was at home. She had quietly sulked for years, her resentment building like a powder keg.

One day the fuse was lit and she exploded, screaming at John and hurling insults. It was nearly four hours before she could stop. John was shocked and distressed. He thought that Elsa enjoyed doing the things that he liked and that she was happy to stay at home. Elsa felt that she deserved better.

Elsa and John went into therapy. Elsa admitted that she felt the sacrifices she made were too great. John said it was Elsa who had volunteered to make them. He was willing for her to put the things she had dropped back into her life again and suggested that they should each take some time out to revitalise.

> Elsa has gone back to work part-time. She has begun to see her family and friends again and the sparkle has come back into her life.

●●●●●●●●●●●●●●●●●●●●●●

## The Sports Addict

Exercise is good for you, but, taken to excess, it can cause problems. There has been a marked increase in complaints by men that their partners are becoming hooked on exercise.

While it is a good idea to join a gym to exercise, when this becomes obsessive, it can affect your relationships as well as being dangerous to you. Exercise releases endorphins which can give you a release of energy and a buzz. When this is taken to excess, you can become hooked on this feeling and stay endlessly at health clubs to work out, to the exclusion of everything else. If you are spending long hours working out in the gym, you could be turning your partner into a Colditz Man.

## Lighten up

All of these personality distortions arise out of irrational beliefs that are based on the assumption that everything that happens to you in life has been 'done' to you by someone else. Of course things do happen to you.

a. You experience something.

b. You then experience an emotion.

c. You express the emotion.

But please note that (a) does not create (c); (b) creates (c). **You**, therefore, create unpleasant emotions.

In their *Relaxation and Stress Reduction Workbook*, Davis, Esselman and Mackay describe how men and women have a tendency to 'awfulise' or 'absolutise'. In my experience, women tend to do this often. They convert ordinary events into total catastrophes and nightmares simply by the way they interpret their experiences. Thus, chest pains can become heart attacks, grumpy au pairs can turn into psychopaths who are leaving the family in despair, and someone failing to say 'Hello' can mean 'I hate you'. People who do this will use the words 'should', 'must' and 'ought', particularly regarding anyone who fails to live up to their standards, but these standards are irrational.

Humans are fallible. If you fail to set a sensible level of failure for yourself and others, you increase your prospects for disappointment and unhappiness. Not only do you create more stress for yourself and others by not doing this – you are more likely to cast blame on others. Studies have found that any party to a conflict is contributing at least 30% of the fuel to keep it going.

It is a waste of energy to constantly battle to discover who did what first. The best strategy is to take steps to change your way of looking at a problem by exchanging irrational views for rational ones (see pp. 37-42).

Try to lighten up and bring some fun back into your relationship. If both of you do this, you will again experience the happiness and contentment which you felt at the start of your relationship.

# CHAPTER 6

# Sex and Relationships

*Men aren't attracted to me by my mind; they are attracted by what I don't mind.*

— Gypsy Rose Lee

In failing relationships, sex is often a source of conflict. Complaints fall into two main categories:

1. Not enough.
2. Too much.

Lack of sex or unhappiness about it is a problem often raised by men in divorce proceedings. For women, emotional issues are primary, with sex as one of the problems way down the list. However, as a divorce lawyer, I find it difficult to discern which comes first – does a diminishing sex life cause a bad relationship or does a bad relationship lead to diminishing sex? In my experience, the answer is 'Both' – to some degree.

Research has been carried out all over the world into the subject of lack of sex and its effect on relationships. In 1982, Reamy found a significant correlation between lack of sex and sexual withdrawal of a female partner and the likelihood of the male partner seeking sex elsewhere. (This study examined the incidence of affairs among married men while their wives were pregnant, however, so other psychological factors may have been involved.)

Still, it is my considered view that lack of sex and/or the unhappiness of the experience has a direct impact on the demise of a relationship.

From the cases I have been involved in, it is clear that, for women, sex is almost always part of a wider emotional experience. For men, emotion may play no part in the physical act of sex. Women generally do not understand how men can have sex and feel no emotion. They tend to resent this and may consequently unwittingly create a problem in their own relationship with their partner.

> *The main problem in marriage is that for a man sex is a hunger like eating. If the man is hungry and can't get to a fancy French restaurant, he goes to a hot dog stand. For a woman, what is important is love and romance.*
>
> – Joan Fontaine

What I have observed is that:

- Women believe that men do not understand their emotional needs before, during and after sex
- Men believe that women do not understand their basic need for sex
- Men generally wish that women would initiate intercourse sometimes and
- Sexual dissatisfaction plays no small part in the creation of Dragon Woman in her many forms.

Men and women have different psychological approaches to sex which, if misunderstood, can cause unhappiness and disappointment. Some of the problems experienced are illustrated by actual cases in this chapter in order to help women understand how men think and act in relation to sex. This may vastly improve their love life. Similarly, men who read this will, I hope, gain a better understanding of what women look for in their sexual encounters. It is only through better understanding that human beings can move towards a more satisfying sex life.

## The Headache Syndrome

So often in divorce proceedings or relationship breakdowns, men describe the same scenario: whenever they try to become sexually close to their partners, they feel they are being rejected. Men have told me that if they try to kiss or massage their partners, or reach out in bed to caress them, they will turn away, act bored or say, 'Not now'. They describe women as behaving 'like sexual robots' – and being frigid and uncaring towards them.

**CASE STUDY** • • • • • • • • • • • • • •

Brian was married to Kate for eight years. At first, their sex life was amazing.

After their children were born, things started to slide downhill. Brian told me that, night after night, after his wife had put the children to sleep, he would try to initiate sex, only to be rebuffed. Kate kept saying things like, 'Maybe tomorrow,' 'Not now' and 'Go away.' Tomorrow never came. He became very resentful and unhappy. He said that when Kate behaved like that, he felt completely rejected, unwanted and unloved. Subsequently suffering what he described as 'a build-up of sexual tension', he became obsessive about sex. Meanwhile Kate kept exploding with Dragon Woman emotion, wanting to talk about her feelings, often telling him 'I don't think you care.' He said that made him even worse! He would reply, 'I'm trying to show you that I care, but you never want sex.'

In their frustration and anger, neither could see the problem clearly. Brian started an affair with Julie at the office and left Kate.

This story is typical of many in divorce cases. Kate

didn't want sex because she felt unattractive after she became a mother, but she couldn't find the right way to express her concerns. Brian would not listen to her emotional outbursts, perceiving them as attacks on him. The truth is, he felt rejected. They became polarised in their feelings of fear and rejection – Dragon Woman being afraid and Colditz Man feeling rejected. If Kate had understood that Brian was trying to communicate with her, in his own way, and if she had allowed him to, he might have opened up to her more emotionally. Instead, she shut him out.

• • • • • • • • • • • • • • • • • • • •

This story highlights a problem that couples often face. Therapists recommend that couples should try to communicate in a non-rejecting way, and suggest trying sex after cuddling first, so that both people might feel more sensuous.

Women often fall into a rut of not wanting sex because they want their partners to touch them and talk to them, particularly about their feelings and emotions, which men can find difficult to do. Sexual psychotherapist Judith Keshet Orr explains that women fetch to a relationship their insecurities and past experiences as well as a template from their own parents for dealing with others' behaviour. When it comes to sex, their past experiences may make women feel particularly insecure. They try to find security through expressing their feelings, which makes men go into 'shut-out mode'. This inevitably leaves insecure women feeling even more insecure. All likelihood of sex soon evaporates.

The reasons for these differences are found in our physiological make-up. Many men are conditioned from birth to suppress their emotions, and to protect and care for women, whereas women are encouraged to express their feelings in order to reassure others. It is little wonder that they are so different in their perspective, particularly with regard to sex.

Men, when they desire sex, often cannot see the need for all the emotional baggage that women bring to it. A woman who feels that she has not received the emotional security that she requires, will reject her partner's advances, because she simply cannot cope with sex without it. This will make him angry and frustrated.

Normally, this will build into a habit where he expects to be rebuffed and refuses to be emotional while she is annoyed about his insensitivity, and even more likely to reject him – and so the cycle continues.

According to Allan and Barbara Pease, authors of *Why Men Don't Listen and Women Can't Read Maps*, the sex centre is located in the hypothalamus, an organ below the brain. In men the hypothalamus is much larger than in women, so their sexual drive is more powerful. Men also have an abundance of the hormone testosterone, which gives them a higher sex drive.

For women, it is psychological factors which create the right conditions to release the hormones that govern sexual drive. The more reassurance they receive, the more relaxed and secure they feel and the more aroused they become. Unfortunately, the greater the woman's need for emotional reassurances the more her partner will be repelled.

*A student undergoing a word association test was asked why a snowstorm had put him in mind of sex. He replied, 'Frankly, because everything does'.*
– Honor Tracy

In such situations, women often blame their partners for being unfeeling and uncaring, and this anger and frustration spills over into their whole relationship. In the divorce cases in which I have been involved, men tell me that they want their wives to respond to their physical advances; when this doesn't happen, they feel rejected. It seems that the more insecure a woman is, the more frustrated she will become in her sexual relationship, unless her partner understands her needs.

I have found that middle-aged women, particularly menopausal women, can create the very situation that they wish to avoid in their relationships. This is because the older the woman, the more reassurance she will need that she is sexy and loved. Her insecurities can overwhelm every aspect of the relationship and prevent any physical intimacy.

**CASE STUDY** ●●●●●●●●●●●●●●●

> Cheryl and Paul had been married for fifteen years. Cheryl had been extremely sexy and attractive in her twenties. As their marriage progressed, Paul found that Cheryl was more likely to reject his sexual advances. The more he tried to persuade her to have sex, the more reluctant she became. Cheryl started to build up a fear of having sex with Paul and Paul built up a fear of rejection.
>
> In the course of therapy, these issues were carefully examined. It transpired that Cheryl was very unhappy about her appearance. She thought Paul found her ugly, and she couldn't come to terms with her fading looks. She couldn't bear the lines that were appearing on her face and thought that Paul would hate her for the way that she had become. Through therapy, she built up her self-esteem and learned that Paul did indeed find her very sexy; that was why he wanted to initiate sex with her. Cheryl's insecurity stemmed from the fact that her father had left her mother for a younger woman. Once she had worked through this, she and Paul were able to talk through their problems together, and their sex life flourished.

●●●●●●●●●●●●●●●●●●●●

If your sex life has started to dwindle and you are caught in the trap of fear and insecurity, take a good look at what is causing the problem. If your partner is unable to discuss emotional issues just before or during sex, don't be angry with him for this. This is a normal response. Ask him to give you a hug first; this will make you feel more reassured without raising all the other emotional issues, and he will start to relax too.

If you feel it is impossible to discuss the issue with him, show him a copy of this chapter and suggest you work together to solve the problem.

## Physical Release vs. Emotion

Many men see sex as a physical release – a way of getting rid of their problems. Sex may not help, but they think it will.

This can make women feel used, so that they start a cycle of rejection. If, however, they can accept that this is how many men deal with their emotions, they may actually help them to do so. For men, sex is a way of feeling close and loving, while women need the build-up to an emotional release. They cannot switch from being a housewife or career woman into a sexual nymphette in mere seconds.

In therapy sessions, men often reveal that they are actually very lonely and unable to express their need for emotional comfort. Some men find it difficult to make friends, and internalise their problems. The only way they can release them safely is through sex.

Therapists suggest that if a woman encourages her partner to open up and talk about his feelings of fear and failure, their sex life will improve dramatically, although the path towards this goal is very rocky and can lead to conflict. A sensitive, understanding woman (www.woman) knows how to achieve this. Create an environment where your man does not feel threatened by emotion, and use language that you know will encourage him to talk. It often helps if you are sexually close at the time.

It is at this point that women have the power to determine whether this closeness turns their friendship into a happier experience or into one polarised by feelings of dread. Saying, 'What's wrong?', 'You don't love me' or 'You don't care about me' will have a detrimental effect on a man's sexual prowess. If, on the other hand, you make him feel approved of and appreciated, you can raise issues about his worries in a positive way. Saying things like, 'It must be difficult for you, waiting to hear about that contract, but I know, whatever the outcome, you've done brilliantly,' will make your partner more likely to respond to and open up to you.

## 1. What Women Want

In divorce proceedings, women often describe their disappointment about men's failure to be emotional and to tune in to their feelings. When it comes to sex, women say this is what they want:

- To talk about the way they feel first
- To be held and cuddled
- To be told they are attractive
- Sex to go slowly
- To be aroused first
- To be kissed and touched
- To feel that they are participating
- To feel that they are making love, not just 'having sex'
- To be pampered
- To feel protected and loved.

Women say that men seem to race ahead, intent on one goal only. The lack of some or all of the above makes them feel rejected and resentful. They also complain that their partners fall asleep after sex or read and become impatient with them if they try to discuss their feelings after sex. They say that this makes them feel used and unhappy. Women obviously want the emotions of sex to linger afterwards and to wallow in the soft afterglow of sexual satisfaction, to be held and cuddled and listened to. Men can't do this. Psychologists suggest that this is because men lose control during sex, and want to reimpose some sort of control afterwards. To men, this is natural. To some women, it spells rejection. But if you understand the reason for your partner's behaviour, you will not be upset by it.

> *After ecstasy, the laundry.*
>
> – Zen saying

## 2. What Men Want

Male clients have told me this is what they want:

- To be rejected less
- Not to be made to feel guilty about wanting sex
- More passion and more spontaneous sex
- Their partner to be more physically active during sex
- Carefree, romping sex occasionally
- Women to understand that their desire often comes from being visually aroused by their partner.

# Foreplay

In divorce cases, men have complained to me that they are expected to concentrate on foreplay to such a degree that it turns them off sexually. They want to be passionate, so sometimes their foreplay can become half-hearted and cursory.

Taking this as a sign that their men aren't interested and can't be bothered, women become frustrated and angry. The www.woman knows that sometimes it is perfectly in order to let your partner's passion take over without the preliminaries of foreplay. She knows if she insists on the whole package every time, he will become resentful, and their lovemaking mechanical.

**CASE STUDY** • • • • • • • • • • • • • •

> Elaine and George had been married for six years. At the beginning they had what George referred to as 'a rampant sex life'. They would have sex regularly and it was always passionate and fulfilling.
>
> After about five years, George found that Elaine's demands were becoming overwhelming. She would take longer and longer to become sexually aroused and would want foreplay to last interminably. Instead of looking forward to sex, the thought of it was now turning George off. His arousal was intense but would soon wane to the extent that he began to think about the next day's bookkeeping entries.
>
> Their sex life slowed, then stopped. After a year of no sex between them, George left Elaine.
>
> If George had told Elaine he enjoyed the spontaneity of sex and wished to please her as well, and Elaine had seen that she was demanding and stultifying, then matters would have been vastly different.

• • • • • • • • • • • • • • • • • • • • • •

Many women in divorce proceedings describe men as selfish lovers because they have a need for spontaneous passion. An ideal sex life is a combination of pleasing your partner and being spontaneous. It's a matter of striking the right balance.

## Talking and Sex

The fact that many women seem unable to stop talking causes problems in many areas of relationships. For men, their endless chatter can be infuriating; during sex it is intolerable.

While men don't mind talking before sex – indeed, they are quite happy to talk for hours if the ultimate result is getting a woman into bed – they don't want to talk during sex itself. There is a physiological reason for this: in men, the right-hand side of the brain controls hand and eye co-ordination and visual abilities, the left-hand side their verbal abilities. Men find it extremely difficult to switch from one to the other. They use one side of their brain for talking and the other for touching and feeling. In order to do one, they have to interrupt the other. This has been likened to taking both hands off the steering-wheel while driving a car. Being required to have a conversation during sex, therefore, will ruin a man's concentration and turn him off.

**CASE STUDY** ● ● ● ● ● ● ● ● ● ● ● ● ● ● ●

> Stephanie and Alex had a very good sex life for two years. After Stephanie started working, she seemed to want to talk about her job all the time, particularly during sex.
>
> Alex was dumbfounded when, at the point of climax, Stephanie asked him: 'Do you think I should put in for a rise now, or wait for a month?' Alex said that he only grunted in response, but it completely put him off and he was furious with her. He thought it was a one-off event, but Stephanie kept bringing things up during sex, until he could take it no more and told her to 'shut up'. However, the more he did this, the more Stephanie talked.
>
> Eventually Alex started an affair with someone else. When Stephanie discovered this, she was furious with Alex. How could he be so unfeeling? Did he want to end their marriage? Alex replied that it was her fault: she had pushed him into it.
>
> When Stephanie said that she really wanted the marriage to work, they went together to see a marriage-guidance counsellor. During therapy, Stephanie's overwhelming urge to talk during sex was highlighted. Stephanie saw for the first time how irritating this was to Alex. They reached an agreement: she wouldn't try to have conversations during sex, and he would allow her all the time she needed to talk afterwards.

● ● ● ● ● ● ● ● ● ● ● ● ● ● ● ● ● ● ● ● ●

# Sexual Hang-ups

From the beginning of time, men have felt at ease with their sexuality. Many women are still uncomfortable with theirs.

If a woman's mother or family have passed on to her a feeling of disgust or guilt about sex, she will bring this with her into any relationship she has with men. Sex therapists believe this is why some women behave as though they just want to get sex over with. During sex they are completely unresponsive, leaving their partners feeling frustrated, guilty and miserable.

In many surveys about sex, men complain that women just lie there, expecting them to do all the work, closing their eyes and 'thinking of England'. This happens for two reasons: the woman is simply not enjoying the sexual act, or she has been led to believe that that is how she is meant to behave. If you are one of these women, don't be frightened about sex. It is perfectly acceptable for you to move about and to enjoy sex.

Men also complain that they always have to initiate sex; they wish their partners would take the initiative and express desire, and make them feel wanted. Many women believe that it is unacceptable for a woman to make the first move – a naïve, old-fashioned idea probably implanted by years of social conditioning. It is time for women to reprogramme themselves – and take the initiative regarding sex. Your partner will love you all the more for it.

A man's ability to satisfy a woman can give a big boost to his ego. Conversely, young, inexperienced women are often frightened of sex and of disappointing their partner, particularly if they were brought up to be unselfish and giving. In these situations, practice makes perfect. The more you experiment, the more you are likely to please. There is nothing wrong in gently asking your partner to tell you what he enjoys. Don't be afraid to tell him what turns you on, but be sure you don't make him feel pressured to perform on command.

Be gentle. Remember: erogenous zones are for stimulation, not assault! (If you find sexual intercourse painful or distressing, it is important to seek medical help.)

# Orgasm

Many men believe that producing orgasms or multiple orgasms in a woman is a measure of their sexual virility. A man becomes extremely frustrated if his partner fails to reach orgasm, or takes a long time to achieve it. Allan and Barbara Pease have found that the average time it takes a healthy man to reach orgasm is two and a half minutes. For a healthy woman, the average is thirteen minutes.

For men to complete the sex act, they must have an orgasm; not all women feel that they necessarily have to. If, however, a woman believes that she has a right to an orgasm and that sex is not complete without it, this may lead to problems. For example, if her partner sees her need as a burden, he may be unable to perform, and suffer from erectile failure. Explaining that not reaching orgasm is not the end of the world will reassure her partner and relieve the pressure on both of them.

# Problems

Men tend to worry about premature ejaculation (reaching orgasm too soon). It leaves them feeling frustrated, and anxious that they have let down their partner. The more experienced the lover, the less likely he is to experience premature ejaculation. He may focus on something boring in order to prevent ejaculation for as long as possible to allow his partner time to reach orgasm.

In a recent survey carried out in London, fifty men were asked to name the image they focused on most frequently in order to prevent premature ejaculation. The following emerged as the top five:

1. Margaret Thatcher

2. Parents having sex

3. Multiplication tables

4. Counting sheep

5. Charles and Camilla

If your sex life has become dull or upsetting, a therapist might suggest reintroducing some fun and frivolity into your relationship, to recapture how it was for you at the beginning of your friendship. Also, try not to make it appear that you are doing your partner a big favour by 'allowing' sex.

Men going through divorce sometimes describe how their wives behave as if they are martyrs, submitting to sex, when it should be a happy experience for both of them. One husband said his wife made him feel that she had to put on gloves to even go near his penis. This did nothing for his self-esteem. If you make your partner aware that you enjoy sex, he will feel good about himself and is likely to be more loving towards you.

## Pornography

In divorce proceedings occasionally, a woman client will complain that she finds her husband's enjoyment of pornography distasteful and disgusting. The fact that men want to look at pornographic magazines or videos does not make them strange or perverted. It is quite normal and does not mean that they prefer the women they see in these films and photographs to their partners. They simply like to look, just as they might admire a new sports car!

If you understand that many men find pornography stimulating, and in some cases helpful, then you will not feel distressed about it. Some women find pornography stimulating, while others regard it as degrading. Whatever your view, show that you understand your partner's need to see it. If you do not wish to join him in looking at such material, communicate this to him in a non-judgmental and non-aggressive way. By doing so, you will avoid an unnecessary and upsetting argument.

## Bullies in the Bedroom

Some Dragon Women, who are used to being in charge at home or at work, can behave in a dominating way in the bedroom. Therapists describe them as bossy, overwhelming and overbearing. They insist on directing operations throughout sexual intercourse. They will not only talk during sex, but bark orders about where they want to be touched – in a way that is extremely off-putting to their partners.

It is important for both parties in a sexual relationship to talk about their desires, however, these should be expressed as preferences and not demands. If you become too domineering, your partner is likely to rebel or switch off.

When women are ignorant about sex or have had a controlling and narrow sexual upbringing, they will be embarrassed about it. They may hide their unease by making offensive jokes about their partners' sexuality, particularly in public. If sex crops up in conversation, they will say things like: 'Well give me a microscope – I'm going to bed with him now.'

**CASE STUDY** * * * * * * * * * * * * * *

> Tim and Clare were married for twelve years. Tim thought that they had a happy sex life. However, in company Clare would constantly deride and belittle him. She would pretend to her friends that she was sexually frustrated, and say she wanted to be thrown on the bed and have wild sex with a real man. She would laugh and joke about

how it would be nice to have a 'bit of rough'. It made Tim
furious. They rowed incessantly and slowly their sex life
evaporated.

∗ ∗ ∗ ∗ ∗ ∗ ∗ ∗ ∗ ∗ ∗ ∗ ∗ ∗ ∗ ∗ ∗ ∗ ∗ ∗ ∗

Men like to feel appreciated and desired. When women talk
to or about them in this way, men feel emasculated. They
tend to regard their penises as objects to be revered. Women
don't actually think of them that way and can even see them
as ridiculous. However jokes about men's sexual performance or penis size are bound to wound them. Many men
believe that penis size determines sexual prowess, even
though it is well known that quality, not quantity, is what is
important in sex.

## Oral Sex

*You know, the worst thing about oral sex is the view.*
                                    – Maureen Lipman

Many women undergoing therapy ask why men like oral sex
so much, as most women are not very concerned about it.
Therapists generally explain that men see their genitalia as a
focal point of their power, sense of purpose and essence.
Many men experience oral sex as the best form of sex, more
arousing than any other. It relieves them of restrictions and
thinking about pleasing their partner. Men are very grateful
to women who give them this opportunity.

Many women find oral sex unpalatable, 'unhygienic' or
sordid. This may be a reflection of their upbringing or a religious or moral stance they have taken. If your partner really
enjoys oral sex, and you want this to be part of your relationship, don't be frightened or revolted; it can be a person's
way of asking for and receiving your total acceptance and
part of a happy, loving relationship.

# Creativity in the Bedroom

Variety is the spice of life and there is nothing that men like more than having variety in sex. This can stimulate and excite them. However, as with everything else in life, moderation is the key to experiencing satisfaction.

**CASE STUDY** ● ● ● ● ● ● ● ● ● ● ● ● ● ◆

David and Sharon had been married for over twenty years. Their sex life was relatively ordinary. But one day Sharon went to the hairdresser's and read a magazine article all about how to spice up your love life. Sharon tore this out, determined to put the information to good use.

David described to me what happened when he came home two days later. As he opened the front door, Sharon attacked him as he came in. She pounced on him, tearing at his clothes and demanding that he make love to her on the stairs. David was flabbergasted. He was not aroused by this – merely shocked. Sharon was deeply disappointed.

Nevertheless, the next day, undeterred, as David came through the front door, Sharon, wearing a negligée, pounced on him again, this time pulling him into the lounge and throwing him on the couch. David was torn between laughing and screaming!

That weekend, as they were making love, Sharon suddenly produced a pot of 'joy jelly' and started slapping it all over David. He was horrified.

Sharon could not understand what she was doing wrong. She had followed the magazine instructions to the letter.

The only thing she had left out was communicating her new ideas to David!

When David left home to move into a hotel for a week, Sharon realised that she had gone too far. She then explained to David that she was not having an affair, as he suspected; neither had she gone mad. She had simply wanted to make sex better for them.

> Once David understood what she was doing, they
> worked as a couple to spice up their sex life, which then
> improved for both of them.

•••••••••••••••••••••••

If you want to be inventive in your sex life, do let your partner know. Otherwise, the shock may cause a heart attack!

## Leave on the Make-up

Men complain endlessly in divorce proceedings that whenever they feel frisky, their wives always have to take off their make-up first. 'Why does it always take so long?' they ask me. They say it takes an age for their partners to cleanse, tone and moisturise, by which time they have lost the will to live! We women know that often it's a device we use when we don't want sex. Women who do, however, may not realise how frustrating it is for a man in the throes of desire to wait.

Wives who divorce their husbands sometimes complain about their husbands being asleep when they come out of the bathroom, leaving them feeling frustrated. If you are one of these women, may I suggest that you have sex first, then take as long as you wish to remove your make-up afterwards. Otherwise, leave off make-up entirely, but do make sure that you look and smell good to your partner.

# CHAPTER 7

# Women and Appearance

*If truth is beauty, how come no one has their hair done in the library?*

– Lily Tomlin

In divorce proceedings, I have discovered that looking good can make a difference to relationships. This does not mean that women must be obsessed with fashion or take concern about their appearance to extremes.

Nor does it mean she should completely ignore one of the fundamental tenets of feminism that a woman should be her own person, free from the oppression imposed upon her by men. Until the early 1960s, most women tailored their appearance to satisfy men, but in the sixties women began to dress to please themselves. Women no longer looked at style in terms of what was likely to be pleasing to men and were actively encouraged to take the view that looks did not matter. Inner, not external, beauty was emphasised. Women everywhere were delighted. At last they could be free from the bondage of always having to look good.

Generally, fashions since the sixties have become steadily less aesthetically pleasing to men. One only has to look at them to see that this is the case. Punk, for instance, arose as part of a street revolution to satisfy some people's desire to appear poor and from the concept that males and females were not only equal but the same. Suddenly androgyny became popular. Such fashions indicate to me that women are projecting their own self-loathing, and are no longer dressing to please men.

There is something unsettling and sad about this and other styles that are intended to shock and revolt. One has only to look at models in magazines and fashion shows to see that they are actively encouraged to dress in an unpleasing way. There was a particular fashion in the nineties where models emulated drug addicts with dark circles under their eyes and sunken cheeks. Styles like Grunge, which I see as throwing together outfits without interest or care, are a barometer for assessing how women feel about themselves, and, perhaps, men and their opinions.

In February, 2000, an article in *Style* magazine included this story:

> *A Mercedes Estate pulls up outside a London shop. 'Can I exchange this outfit?' asks a 30-something woman, poking her head around the door. 'My husband really hates it.'*
> *'Of course,' says the shop owner, writing out a credit note.*
>
> *'Pathetic,' she says, as the woman retreats. 'Don't you feel sorry for people who dress for men? I don't ask my husband's opinion. Heaven knows what he would like me to wear.'*

So whom do women dress for? Some of the career women I know say that sometimes they dress for themselves, occasionally they dress for men, but mostly, in business, they dress to out-do other women.

According to Colin McDowell, in his *Directory of 20th Century Fashion*, a fashionable person sees fashion as a way of telling the world of his or her success, importance, attraction and desirability. Clothes can be used not only as the trappings of power but part of the exercise of power itself to frighten and intimidate others into submission. These inspire awe and envy and, in some, feelings of inferiority.

'Clothes', says McDowell, 'are a form of social and political commentary and are a uniform for those who wish to stand outside of society, which they find inadequate and negative.' He seeks to explain the decline in some women's mode of dress thus: 'Elegance and glamour are almost taboo because they are not only elitist; they are considered dangerous.'

So where do men fit into all of this?

Men are visual creatures and they like to look at things that are visually pleasing – far more than women do. Men also like to look at women.

As a divorce lawyer, I can say with absolute authority that all of my male clients have told me:

1. Women's looks do matter to men.
2. The fact that men look at women does not mean that they want to be with them or have sex with them. Often they don't even realise that they are staring at a woman. They just like to see women with good looks.
3. Men like to look at women's bodies in magazines, films and videos.

## Looking Good

Women often complain about having to look good for their overweight, pot-bellied, middle-aged husbands. 'Why doesn't he have to look good for me?' they ask. 'Why is men's grey hair distinguished, while ours is unacceptable?' The answer is, 'That's life!'

> *I live by a man's code, designed to fit a man's world, yet at the same time I never forget that women's first job is to choose the right shade of lipstick.*
> – Carole Lombard

The unfortunate truth is that a woman's appearance does matter to her partner and can affect their relationship. In divorce proceedings, particularly where men have started affairs or are leaving home because of affairs, men's reasons for turning away from their wives are often connected with this.

In a survey I conducted in 1999, I asked eighty men who had committed adultery to set out their reasons for being disloyal, in order of priority. One of the most common reasons given was: 'My wife had started to look and sound like her mother.' The men interviewed told me that before they got married, their wives were sexy and cared about their looks. Afterwards, they did not seem to pay attention to them and let themselves go. When these men came home from work, having spent the day surrounded by coiffured and elegant ladies, these men would be greeted by a wife wearing a dressing-gown or leggings, and smudged make-up or no make-up at all. This, coupled with a hostile, uncaring attitude emanating from their wives, had turned them into Colditz Men who longed to reverse back out the front door.

> *Not every woman in old slippers can manage to look like Cinderella.*
>
> – Don Marquis

**CASE STUDY** ◆◆◆◆◆◆◆◆◆◆◆◆◆◆

Henry had been married to Alice for ten years. They both worked, and they had two children. Henry told me that, when he first met Alice, she was 'the sexiest woman on earth'. He particularly loved her legs, which were slim and attractive. He felt she dressed for him in elegant skirts and he was proud to be seen with her.

After six years of marriage, however, every time he came home, he would find Alice in the same old dressing gown. She looked as if she had been dragged through a hedge backwards, he said. She had become a typical Dragon Drone – angry, aggressive and stressed. Clearly unhappy with herself, she had put on an enormous amount of weight. The larger she became, the more aggressive her manner became.

Henry couldn't understand why Alice dressed for work with care, but didn't seem concerned about what she looked like for him. Since she left for work after and came back home before Henry, he never had an opportunity to see her looking good.

Weekends were the same. For evenings out with friends, Alice rarely made an effort, hardly ever putting on make-up, and he began to feel uncomfortable about the way she looked.

He felt that the fact that she was neglecting her appearance meant that she had stopped caring about him. He explained that, even if she made an effort to appear presentable, somehow, midway through the evening, she would start to look a wreck. 'Other women went to the ladies to check their make-up or rearrange their hair,' Henry said, 'but she never did.' His wife's appearance made him feel bad, but he felt guilty about harbouring these thoughts, which he suppressed for over four years.

Then he met a woman at work who seemed to understand the way he felt. She was attractive and he felt good being with her. He left Alice.

Alice was heartbroken when Henry left her. Afterwards, she lost two stone, and spent about six months taking a close look at her life.

She started to wear make-up again and to take care with her appearance. Then she met and fell in love with Bill, to whom she is now happily married.

Alice underwent what is known as a 'break-over': a change in appearance that occurs as a direct consequence of a broken relationship. This frequently happens in such situations, but often too late to save relationships.

• • • • • • • • • • • • • • • • • • • •

The Henry and Alice scenario is, unhappily, a very familiar one. Many men like to feel proud of the way their partner looks. The fact that a man's wife is fat is not, in itself, the reason why he divorces her; it is what surrounds her loss of looks that repels him. A man feels that if his partner makes an effort with her appearance (regardless of her size), it reflects the level of regard that she has for him. If she doesn't bother, he doesn't feel she cares for him.

Women cannot understand why men think this way. If a woman loves a man, she will love him whatever he looks like. This is because a woman is far more attracted by a man's personality, charm and humour than his looks.

Men, on the other hand, generally are attracted by looks first and charm and humour second. Although, for a long-term relationship, men are concerned about a woman's intelligence, humour, etc., the first thing that attracts them is a woman's physical attractiveness.

> *Dressing up, for me, is not an effort. And if you live with someone, it is a courtesy to look as good as you can.*
> – Paloma Picasso

I am not suggesting that you should never be caught looking untidy or without make-up. However, never making an effort to look good can have a detrimental effect on your relationship, because your partner may infer that you don't care about him. So look after your appearance. Don't always appear a mess when you see him and occasionally wear something really sexy, just to please him.

> *The average girl would rather have beauty than brain because she knows the average man can see much better than he can think.*
> – Anon

# Dress to Kill

It is no excuse to claim that you are too fat or too thin to find the right things to wear, although it is a fact of life that not everyone has dress sense. Some women have no notion of colour co-ordination, what suits them, what patterns can clash and which styles are most flattering to their figures. But it is not difficult, or expensive, to become better informed. Fashion tips can be found in newspapers, magazines and books, and via radio and television programmes. If you can afford it, get advice from a personal shopper in a good department store. They will help you choose the colours and clothes that suit you best. A free make-over can teach you how to apply the right make-up, and you can tint your hair at home if you are short of funds.

It is a myth that only the most expensive clothes make a woman look good. It is how you wear your clothes that makes the difference. Even the most expensive outfit can look dreadful if it is too tight, creased or clashes with your hair. There are numerous factory outlets that sell beautiful clothes at a discount. Most of them are open seven days a week, so lack of time to shop is no excuse either. Don't be too frightened to experiment. Have confidence in yourself.

> *All God's children are not beautiful – most of God's children are, in fact, barely presentable.*
>
> – Fran Lebowitz

# Turn-offs

In divorce proceedings, men often tell me that certain matters really upset them, apart from their partners putting on weight, ignoring their appearance and becoming bossy and overbearing. They say that they would not mind these so much if their partners showed they were making an effort by at least attending to their looks and hygiene. Many British men are repelled, for instance, by hairy women – i.e., those with an excess of facial or body hair. They do not like chipped, broken nails, or false nails if some are missing. Nor do they like cloying, overwhelming perfume or unchecked body odour. They abhor rough feet and long, scratchy toenails. While this is bad news for women, it is good news for beauticians.

> *There are no ugly women, only lazy ones.*
>                                        – Helena Rubinstein

Many women believe that a man should love them regardless of their hairy legs and broken nails. They become infuriated at the mere suggestion that men should impose such ridiculous standards upon them. However, if you think your grooming may be less than perfect, and may be affecting your relationship, you have two choices:

1. Ignore the problem and take the consequences, or
2. Do something about it, thereby enhancing and protecting your relationship.

Neglecting yourself indicates to your partner that you do not care about him. These days it is easy to obtain depilatory creams and beauty products, even at the supermarket. If you can afford it, arrange to visit a beautician for a manicure or pedicure; she may even come to your home if you are short of time.

**CASE STUDY** ●●●●●●●●●●●●●●●●

Patricia and Max had been married for eight years when Max noticed that Patricia was starting to neglect her appearance. She would rarely shave her legs and her moustache became more and more pronounced. Max found himself becoming very irritated by this. When they went out with friends and Patricia wore a skirt, Max imagined that everyone was staring at the hair on her legs, which made her look masculine and unattractive.

When they went on holiday, Patricia was always hot and sweaty, and she developed an unpleasant odour. By the evening, it was very strong. When they went to bed, Max told me, Patricia rarely showered or bathed beforehand and her body odour would totally repel him. He didn't want to make love and couldn't wait to get away from her.

Eventually their sex life died altogether and consequently they went into therapy together. It was there that Patricia was made aware of her problem. At first, she was deeply embarrassed and ashamed, and it made matters worse, but after a while she realised that she had to address the situation. When she did so, with expert help, they were able to resurrect their sex life and their marriage was saved.

● ● ● ● ● ● ● ● ● ● ● ● ● ● ● ● ● ● ● ● ● ●

Many people do not realise that they have a body-odour problem. Because it is such an embarrassing subject, partners may be too scared to raise the issue. As part of your hygiene programme, it is sensible to have a shower or bath before you go to bed. (If the body-odour problem persists, it may be advisable to consult a doctor.)

# Green-eyed Monsters

*Jealousy, that dragon which slays love under the pretence of keeping it alive.*

– Havelock Ellis

Women are irritated by men who spend a lot of time leering at women. Such men are, they believe, flawed. A Fiat Punto advert that appeared in Britain in late 1999 encapsulates this:

*A woman is driving a Fiat Punto with a man in the
passenger seat. He looks at every girl who walks by, even
craning his neck to get a better view of an especially pretty
one. His companion, a woman driver, is becoming increasingly angry. Finally she stops the car, beckons a
good-looking stranger and kisses him enthusiastically upon
the mouth. Her passenger is dumbfounded. Then he smiles
and says, 'Oh, I see, no more looking!'*

Given that men will do this sort of thing, women must
understand what is happening. I am sure that there is no
woman alive who has not wanted to throw something over
her partner at a party, disco, restaurant or on vacation
because he is staring at or paying too much attention to
another woman. Men do this because they are programmed
to; it is an instinctive trait.

Women become annoyed about this because we are basic
-ally insecure creatures who are concerned that our bodies
should constantly be seen as attractive by our partners.
When men look at other women, it suggests to us that they
find those women more attractive than us, and thus perpet-
uates our insecurities.

Statistics show that relationships are twice as likely to
break down during holidays than at any other time. The
reason for this is that women's insecurity levels are highest
then. One look or word that suggests that a woman is not the
most attractive person in a crowd can trigger her worst insecurities. Since men will stare at women preening themselves
on beaches and elsewhere, all of them as insecure as each
other, holidays are disasters just waiting to happen.

Until recently, I spent most of such times seething. Then
I realised that life is to be enjoyed, and it's acceptable for men
to get pleasure from looking.

Now I point out the really beautiful women to my

husband before he spots them. When I do, he just laughs and tells me that he finds me much more attractive. Even if he is lying, it still makes me feel good.

> *When a man takes an interest in a woman's body, she accuses him of only taking an interest in her body, but when he doesn't take an interest in her body, she accuses him of taking an interest in someone else's body.*
>
> – P. J. O'Rourke

## Nips and Tucks

Some women are obsessed about looking beautiful to men and can take it to extremes, having all of their less attractive body parts surgically moulded until they are perfect. Although British women have not yet succumbed to the body-sculpting epidemic sweeping the USA, the trend is growing.

**CASE STUDY** ●●●●●●●●●●●●●●●

A client of mine, Jeremy, had been married to Joanna for twelve years.

When she reached the age of 40, he told me, Joanna felt that she was on a downward slide. She booked herself in for a breast-augmentation operation to enlarge her bust. Then she had a nose job to ensure that it was pert and upturned. Next, she had a tummy-tuck, followed by the removal of the bags under her eyes. Finally, she had a face-lift.

Jeremy was not only horrified at the expense involved, but concerned about the fact that all of it was so unnecessary. He said that Joanna was very pretty and that he loved her looks just as they were. He was unhappy that she wanted to change them. He said that he used to love the feel of Joanna's breasts, but now they felt like rocks. He was frightened to touch her 'in case any of her bits fell off', he told me.

> Jeremy said that Joanna became so self-obsessed that there was no one else left in the relationship. So he walked out. Joanna was upset when Jeremy left her, but said she felt that she had outgrown him!

• • • • • • • • • • • • • • • • • • • • •

Some women can become so addicted to cosmetic surgery that they actually repel their partners. They can then become so self-obsessed that no one is good enough for them.

In all things in life, moderation is the key. The www.woman understands that a balance must be struck between trying to make her partner happy with her appearance and going to extremes. Glad that her looks please her partner, she is prepared to put extra effort into making the most of what she has and is. Are you?

# CHAPTER 8

# Help! The Hormonal Dragons Are Coming…

*If men could menstruate, clearly menstruation would become an enviable, boastworthy masculine event. Men would bray about how long and how much, sanitary supplies would be federally funded and free, of course. Some men would still pay for the prestige of such commercial brands as 'Paul Newman Tampons', 'Muhammed Ali's Rope-a-Dope-Pads', 'John Wayne Maxi Pads' and 'Joe Namath Jock Shields' for those light bachelor days.*

— Gloria Steinem

Is your love-life sinking under the waves whipped up by your own internal storms? Does the moon periodically transform you into a Dragon Woman in one or all of her guises? Or could it be your hormones?

You may be wondering why a divorce lawyer should be talking about hormones. It is because hormonal imbalance directly affects relationships and gives rise to serious problems that bring people to me and the divorce courts. Because the subject is still relatively misunderstood, couples often sweep it under the carpet until severe symptoms crash through their tolerance barrier. It is at this stage that my help is asked for. It is because so many women refuse to deal with their hormonal problems that their relationships can and do founder. A hormonal imbalance can adversely affect relationships when:

1. The woman suffers from severe pre-menstrual tension (or pre-menstrual syndrome);
2. She has post-natal depression; or
3. She is going through the menopause.

## PMT and PMS

Pre-menstrual tension (PMT) or pre-menstrual syndrome (PMS) is caused by a hormonal imbalance that is related to a variety of external factors; 60 to 75 per cent of all women of child-bearing age suffer from one or more of its symptoms. Since women spend half of their lives in a menstrual cycle, it is something which must and should be understood.

Pre-menstrual syndrome describes a collection of mental and physical symptoms which occur pre-menstrually. They begin a few days to a week before menstruation and then slowly diminish. Sometimes they occur mid-cycle and disappear, only to recur pre-menstrually. In some women, symptoms continue on into menstruation.

> *When people say women can't be trusted because they cycle every month, my response is that men cycle every day, so they should only be allowed to negotiate peace treaties in the evening.*
> – June Reinisch (1992)

'Pre-menstrual tension' was the name given to the condition by Dr. Frank in the 1930s, but later, Dr. Katerina Dalton, a leading expert on the subject, renamed it 'pre-menstrual syndrome' or PMS. Following are symptoms connected with PMS.

Acne

Agoraphobia

Anxiety

Asthma

Backache

Bad breath

Bloating

Boils

Clumsiness

Confusion

Constipation

Cramping pains

Craving for food

Crying

Cystitis

Depression

Diarrhoea

Disorientation

Dizziness

Eczema

Excessive thirst

Fainting

Fatigue

Forgetfulness

Generalised aches

Hayfever

Headache

Heart palpitations

Heavy, aching legs

Hives

Hostility

Increased physical activity

Insomnia

Irritability

Loss of interest in sex

Migraine

Mood swings

Mouth ulcers

Nervous tension

Painful joints

Restlessness

Sensitivity to light

Sensitivity to noise

Sugar cravings

Swollen abdomen

Swollen ankles

Swollen breasts

Swelling of extremities

Tender/sore breasts

Thoughts of suicide

Tremors and shakes

Weight gain

Wind

At least 150 symptoms are associated with PMS. These hormonal changes can be brought on by a variety of external contributing factors, including:

a. Problems with relationships, children, family, friends or partners

  b. Problems at work

  c. Lack of sleep

  d. Financial problems

  e. Inadequate or poor diet

  f.  Childbirth

  g. Lack of exercise

  h. Operations or physical illnesses.


Unhappy relationships can cause a hormone imbalance, which in turn causes pre-menstrual syndrome and its own behavioural problems. Obviously this can promote a cycle in which relationships suffer.

Reports show that women aged 18 to 24 are likely to have more painful periods and to suffer from pre-menstrual tension brought on by stress. Those in the 25 to 39 age group are most likely to suffer from PMT, lack of energy and painful periods, while those aged 40 to 49 are least likely to suffer from PMT. Studies have found that women who are under stress are likely to complain about PMT and lack of energy, and that there is a direct link between women who suffer from stress and those who suffer from PMT.

> *Menstruation is not a disease, nor should it reduce a*
> *woman to a state of even slight temporary invalidism.*
> – E. B. Duffy

In one of the most far-reaching studies on the subject, Dr. Guy Abrahams identified four types of pre-menstrual syndrome (some women suffer from all of them). After extensive research, Dr. Abrahams found links between certain nutritional deficiencies and these types of PMS. They are, broadly, as follows:

| | |
|---|---|
| **PMS – A** | Anxiety, nervous tension, mood swings and irritability. |
| DEFICIENCIES | A lack of vitamin B$^6$ and magnesium. |
| **PMS – H** | Hormonal weight gain, bloating, swelling and breast tenderness. |
| DEFICIENCIES | A combination of stress, lack of magnesium and vitamins B$^6$ and E. |
| **PMS – C** | Cravings for special foods, desire for sweets, problems with headaches, heart palpitations, tiredness, dizziness or fainting. |
| DEFICIENCIES | Essential fatty acids, vitamin B$^6$, magnesium and chromium. |
| **PSM – D** | Depression, forgetfulness, crying, spells of confusion and sleeplessness. |
| DEFICIENCIES | Most likely to be due to environmental factors, a deficiency in minerals and a dietary imbalance. |

In order to alleviate the symptoms of PMT, he advised women to:

- Eat a healthy diet.
- Examine their intake of vitamins and minerals.
- Avoid or reduce stress.
- Eat fewer sweet foods.
- Change from consuming full- to low-fat dairy produce.
- Drastically reduce or eliminate their intake of coffee, alcohol and animal fats.
- Stop or cut down on smoking.

For those who wish to learn more about PMS, you will find suggestions for further reading at the end of this book, which only offers a basic grounding in how hormone imbalances can affect relationships.

Women's bodies are governed by a spontaneous bio-chemical 22–28-day cycle, during which hormones are released that trigger physical and emotional responses. Women feel their best from the onset of their menstrual cycle until they ovulate. Ovulation is the process whereby an egg leaves the ovaries. This usually takes place about 12 to 16 days before menstruation, and is the time when women bleed. During the first part of the cycle, women may experience happy, positive feelings. At ovulation, their bodies secrete volatile hormones into the air which draw men to them. This coincides with the growth of the egg and the body releases a hormone known as oestrogen.

After ovulation, women secrete progesterone, which is a depressant and has a calming effect. This is when women suffer their worst moods, and hormonal imbalances cause emotional upheavals.

Women who suffer from PMT are usually found to have low progesterone levels and it is for this reason that many treatments involve an increase, either natural or synthetic, of this hormone. Low oestrogen levels cause depression; high oestrogen levels cause anxiety, irritability and tension. The correct levels of oestrogen make women assertive, motivated and emotionally stable.

Where do these hormones come from? Hormones are produced by the ovaries, adrenal glands and thyroid glands. The ovaries produce the sex hormones oestrogen and progesterone; the adrenal glands produce both sex hormones and those related to stress; and the thyroid produces its own hormones and controls metabolism.

These three are controlled by the part of the brain known

as the pituitary gland. Dr. Dorothy Hall refers to this gland as 'the conductor of the hormonal orchestra'. This 'master gland' at the base of the brain secretes hormones that regulate appetite, eating and sleeping rhythms, and the menstrual cycle. The pituitary gland, in turn, is influenced by stress and emotion. This is why external stresses can influence hormonal secretions and therefore one's sense of well-being and moods. When an imbalance occurs, internally or externally, the entire body is disturbed.

PMS sufferers often have low self-esteem or feelings of overwhelming insecurity, and are, therefore, very sensitive and easily emotionally upset. This means that they are predisposed towards negative thoughts and, of course, fundamental to the treatment of PMS is the conversion of negative into positive thoughts.

Those with PMS suffer symptoms very similar to women under stress (highlighted in Chapters 3 and 4). The symtoms are interchangeable, as are the cures. Stress will clearly cause or exacerbate PMS, and the emotional impact upon you and your family will also be the same. Like stress, a poor diet is likely to exacerbate or cause PMS.

Sufferers of PMS-A (anxiety, etc.) can go through a complete wave of personality changes. There has been much in the media about such women committing crimes like assault or shoplifting. Some sufferers develop uncontrollable feelings of violence and aggression, and lash out at those closest to them. Their behaviour tends to be quite out of character and can have disastrous consequences.

**CASE STUDY** • • • • • • • • • • • • • •

> When Catherine and Peter came to see me, they had been married for 16 years.
>
> Two weeks before every period, Catherine would have a mood swing. She would become enraged at the slightest thing. If Peter suggested that they visit his

parents while she was in this mood, she would start to throw things across the room. She seemed to hate the world and everything in it. Peter described how, when she was talking to a friend on the phone, she often slammed down the receiver if her friend said the slightest thing to which she might take exception. She would forget to do the shopping and her rages, directed at him, were legendary in the street where they lived. Peter told me that he knew the moment he came home if she was in this mood. She would pick on him for no reason and slam his food down on the table. If he said anything that irritated her, she would fly into a rage. She often hit him with things she was holding. Once it was a spoon, another time a plate. On one occasion, she was holding a knife, he told me, and he was terrified.

Catherine refused to believe that there was anything wrong with her. Peter could not communicate with her and nor could anyone else. Catherine thought that the whole world was against her. Eventually, Peter could not take any more and left her.

It was after divorce proceedings had begun that Catherine went to see her doctor for depression. During that visit, she confided in him that she and Peter were getting a divorce and showed a copy of the divorce petition to him. Catherine was fortunate that her doctor was intuitive and intelligent. He told her that, judging from the allegations set out in the petition, she might be suffering from pre-menstrual syndrome. He asked Catherine to look carefully in her diary and to work out whether the events about which Peter was complaining fell approximately one week before her periods. She discovered that they did. He recommended that she change her diet and start to take high doses of vitamin $B^6$. Catherine did so, and her symptoms gradually disappeared. Eight months after their separation and just before the decree nisi was issued, Catherine telephoned Peter and told him that she was feeling much better. She explained how the doctor had helped her, and admitted that she had been blind to the effect of her behaviour on their family. She said that when she was pre-menstrual, she felt a sense of absolute desolation, emptiness and despair, and often fantasised about going back to college.

Peter was confused and unhappy. He didn't really want a divorce, he told her, but her failure to do anything about her problems had triggered him to instigate proceedings.

Peter and Catherine were reconciled. Catherine went back to college and she now maintains a balanced diet and a sensible fluid intake, and takes vitamin supplements. Her pre-menstrual symptoms have never recurred, and she and Peter are now happily married.

● ● ● ● ● ● ● ● ● ● ● ● ● ● ● ● ● ● ● ● ●

In her book, *Women's Bodies, Women's Wisdom*, Dr. Christiane Northrup suggests that many women do not realise what their bodies are trying to tell them pre-menstrually. The feelings of low self-esteem that emerge during bouts of PMS should be listened to, and any other symptoms treated, in order to alleviate the problem. Combining dietary changes with stress-reducing techniques is often the key to dealing with PMS.

**CASE STUDY** ● ● ● ● ● ● ● ● ● ● ● ● ● ●

Angela was well aware that she suffered from PMS. Each month it was the same. A week before her period, she became very anxious, magnifying every worry out of all proportion. She would come home from work and agonise all night about some problem at the office.

Meanwhile, her husband, Sidney, had to listen. Sidney began to dread every fourth week, when he knew she would go 'off her head', as he put it. She wouldn't let him sleep, mulling over the latest drama she had invented. Try as he might to persuade Angela to seek help, Sidney simply could not get her to agree. He spoke to her parents, her sister and her doctor, but Angela refused to accept that she was in any way to blame. She told anyone who tried to talk to her about it that Sidney was

unsympathetic about her problems.
    After five years of marriage, Sidney left Angela and
they divorced. To this day, Sidney dreads collecting the
children when Angela is pre-menstrual.

• • • • • • • • • • • • • • • • • • • •

Interestingly, Dr. Dalton has found that it is usually the
husbands or boyfriends of PMS sufferers who make
appointments for their partners to obtain help. Like Angela,
many women refuse to accept there is anything wrong with
them. Or they may believe their problem will simply go away
of its own accord, so it's acceptable to ignore it, little realising that their behaviour is extremely upsetting to their
families.

Sufferers of PMT – C (cravings, headaches, etc.), which is
usually caused by stress, are often working women. Many of
them start the day without breakfast, smoking cigarettes
instead, and drink endless amounts of tea and coffee. As a
result, their energy levels drop, they become nervous and
develop headaches and cravings and more easily fall prey to
PMT.

Their partners describe them as being under a black
cloud, struggling with overwhelming feelings of despair,
often eating compulsively. Such mood swings are so difficult
to deal with that many men find it easier to leave their wives
or girlfriends.

When women suffer from stress, they tend to become
depressed, which may set off a habit of eating junk food.
Cravings for cakes and biscuits come from the lack of
balance in their diets, which are likely to increase their
symptoms of despair and lack of energy. They seem to hate
everyone, become clumsy, and often lose all desire for sex.
Caught in a spiral of stress, PMS and reduced libido, they
push their partners further and further away. Simply reintro-

ducing a proper diet and reducing their stress levels could make their problems recede or disappear altogether.

There has been a marked increase in the numbers of women suffering from PMS in the last twenty years. This is not only because of its high profile in the media. Women's bodies are not built to deal with the present-day stresses created by working and other factors. We are consuming huge amounts of refined and processed foods that contain no nutrients. Many foods also contain hormones and antibiotics. Women, particularly those in Britain, America and Australia, generally do not consume sufficient vegetables and fruit necessary for a balanced diet. I would therefore recommend that, if you suffer from PMS, you make the positive changes to your life outlined in this book.

## Post-Natal Depression

This is a form depression that is suffered by many women after childbirth. As many as 80 per cent of women experience 'the Baby Blues' for up to two weeks after giving birth. Of these, 10 to 15 per cent go on to have some form of mood disorder, expressed as either panic attacks or major depression. Specialists have found that if a woman has a history of depression, she is more at risk of developing post-natal depression and that, having experienced it once, she is likely to experience it again after subsequent births.

Women with moderate to severe PMT are also more likely to suffer from post-natal depression. Emotional factors can play a part: post-natal depression can be made worse if a woman has a feeling of failure or disappointment, perhaps about giving birth. In many cases, it has been found that unfinished problems concerning families, particularly regarding mothers or fathers, create problems. When they have a baby, many women long to be close to their families and partners. If something in one of these significant relationships is lacking, a woman may feel a profound sense of loss or grief. Often women with post-natal depression are totally exhausted, desperately short of sleep and too stressed to cope with their home, partner or baby.

It is vital to pay attention to these symptoms. If you are experiencing these feelings, then it is likely that you will feel unloved, uncared for and unable to cope, and that you will wish to push your partner away. My strong recommendation to you is that you should not think about instigating divorce proceedings or ending a relationship at this time.

If you have recently given birth and feel tired, depressed and unloved, and your relationship is suffering, take a step back. Do not act in haste and instigate divorce proceedings. There is every likelihood that you have post-natal depression, in which case you must seek proper medical help.

**CASE STUDY** • • • • • • • • • • • • • •

> Penny had been married to Roger for ten years. She suffered from PMS and, after the birth of their first child, she had very severe post-natal depression.
>
> Three weeks after the birth of her second child, the same symptoms reappeared: she felt tired, anxious and unable to cope. She blamed Roger, saying he didn't help or care about her. It was clear to all the family that Penny was suffering from another bout of post-natal depression. Again, the symptoms were very severe. She was confused, agitated and could not sleep.
>
> Two months later, Penny left Roger and instructed a solicitor to issue a petition for divorce on the grounds of his unreasonable behaviour. Roger was distraught. In the divorce petition, Penny said that Roger was unfeeling, uncaring and never helped. In fact, Roger was taking their eldest child to school every morning and collecting her, and had undertaken a lot of the housework for a period of four weeks until they employed an au pair. He also came home every lunchtime to see Penny. Regrettably, Penny's lawyer did not question whether there was any other

underlying cause to Penny's unhappiness.

Three months into the process, Penny collapsed. She sought medical help and was diagnosed as suffering from post-natal depression.

On advice, she brought a halt to the divorce proceedings, changed her diet and started taking vitamin B supplements. Within six months, Penny's symptoms were gone.

Roger and Penny were reconciled and are happily married to this day.

* * * * * * * * * * * * * * * * * * * * * *

Dr. Dalton suggests that most women should not be allowed to divorce until at least one year after giving birth. She has even offered to lecture The Law Society on the issue of post-natal depression and the feelings that it can generate.

## The Menopause

> *What happens during the climacteric (the Change) is that the people [a woman] has served all of her life stop making demands on her. She becomes a moon without a nurse. What she wants is to be wanted and nobody wants her.*
>
> – Germaine Greer

This is the time when women make the transition from being fertile to being infertile. Ovulation ceases, as does menstruation, and oestrogen levels fall.

Inside a woman are two ovaries which contain a number of immature eggs known as follicles. Most follicles do not develop into mature eggs, but all make a small amount of oestrogen. A minute contribution from each of these thousands of follicles adds up to a large amount of oestrogen within the woman's body.

As she ages, there is a progressive loss of these follicles; they die off at the rate of thousands per month. By the time a woman reaches her mid-forties, there are only about a thousand left. By the time she reaches her late forties or early fifties, they virtually disappear and, with them, oestrogen. Her periods become lighter and less regular.

This drop in oestrogen levels is known as the Peri-Menopause, and usually beings in a woman's mid-forties and lasts until menopause when menstruation stops. This generally happens between the ages of 48 and 53. Sometimes both occur earlier.

## 1. Symptoms

When oestrogen levels fall, a woman may feel very tired, and experience these symptoms:

Anxiety

Dry vagina

Headaches

Hot flushes

Irritability

Loss of interest in sex

Itchiness of the skin

Insomnia

Loss of memory

Loss of confidence and self-esteem

Mood changes

Night sweats

Painful sex

Given that oestrogen levels fall in most women by approximately 80 per cent at the onset of the menopause, it is not surprising that it causes hormonal imbalances.

## CASE STUDY • • • • • • • • • • • • • •

Paula had been married for twenty years. A typical
Dragon Drone, she had been active and happy, but when
she turned 53, things started to change. She became
anxious and aggressive, and suffered from hot flushes
and insomnia. She would run upstairs and forget why she
had done so.

She felt very tired and angry with the world. She would
shout at her husband, George, for the slightest thing. She
was forever criticising her daughter Samantha, who, at
19, was very pretty and vibrant. George noticed that,
particularly when Samantha was dressed up to go out,
Paula would snap at her and find any excuse to stop her
going out. Paula found it impossible to concentrate and
during conversations would forget names and lose her
train of thought. This made her even angrier, and she
took her feelings out on George.

Paula took no exercise. She sat around eating cakes
and put on dramatic amounts of weight. When Samantha
suggested to Paula that perhaps she might be
menopausal, her mother exploded. She threw several of
their best plates against the wall, then stormed out, and
drove around aimlessly for hours.

After a few months, Paula gave up her job. She just
stayed home, miserable and unhappy.

While her sex life with George had never been regular,
now it disappeared altogether. She simply did not want
sex anymore.

This went on for another year. Paula became worse –
surlier and more depressed. The whole household was
affected. Every time George tried to discuss the issue
with her, she snapped at him, refusing to admit there was
a problem.

Then George met June at the Golf Club. She seemed
warm and understanding. George left home and divorced
Paula.

• • • • • • • • • • • • • • • • • • • •

Paula was clearly suffering terribly from the effects of the menopause. Had she agreed to address her problems, her marriage could and would have been saved.

While some men are unsympathetic when their partners are undergoing hormonal changes, there are many who do understand and want to help. It is often a woman who puts her relationship with her husband and family at risk by her refusal to see that she has a problem or do anything about it.

If you recognise that you are suffering from any of these symptoms, then do something to counteract their effects.

### a. Hot Flushes

Sensations of intense warmth, these are 'personal heat-waves' which can cause a woman's neck, head and upper body to turn bright pink. (As a result of the drop in oestrogen levels, the heart races and blood vessels open to push more blood to the surface of the skin.) Heavy perspiration may be followed by chills and shivering. A hot flush can last anywhere from a few seconds to two minutes. These are sometimes called 'night sweats' because they happen at night.

### b. Mood Swings

As their oestrogen levels fluctuate, many women become irritable, moody and anxious, and have trouble concentrating. They may become further depressed because of external changes that are happening in their lives. Their children may leave home, for example, leaving them feeling a great sense of loss.

### c. Disrupted Sleep

Insomnia and its consequent fatigue are usually the result of night sweats. Over a period of time, sleep disturbances can cause memory lapses, anxiety and further fatigue.

### d. Vaginal Dryness

As oestrogen levels go down, the tissues lining the vaginal walls thin and dry out. The resulting lack of natural lubrication can make intercourse very uncomfortable for some women. Creams and herbal treatments can help, however.

### e. Sexual Problems

Some women begin to have sexual problems during the menopause. If they acknowledge that it is a natural stage of life, and know that help is available, any problems can be alleviated and happy sexual relationships restored.

Those whose sex lives were unhappy before the menopause will probably find that they do not improve, however. In addition, women with low self-esteem are more likely to suffer from menopausal symptoms which will also affect their sexual relationships.

## 2. Solutions

Menopause is neither a disease nor an oestrogen-deficiency disorder. It is a natural phase of life marked by falling oestrogen levels. Any symptoms these cause can easily be alleviated. It is important to note that there are many alternatives to taking HRT that may be used to deal with the problems encountered during menopause.

### a. Hormone Replacement Therapy

In hormone replacement therapy (HRT), women take synthetic hormones (principally oestrogen) to supplement or replace those lost during menopause; this sometimes alleviates the adverse effects of menopause. HRT can be given in various forms: as pills, adhesive patches, creams or implants. Oestrogen is often prescribed in combination with progesterone.

Much has been written on the advantages and disadvantages of HRT. It is up to an individual to decide, in consultation with her doctor, whether to take it. Women who are suffering from severe menopausal symptoms, provided there are no contrary indications to HRT, may benefit greatly from it. Their relationships will benefit, too.

## b. Dietary Changes and Exercise

It has been found that women suffering from severe menopausal problems have an inadequate diet and/or exercise too little, so it is important to eat plenty of vegetables in order to obtain natural oestrogens from phytoestrogens and isoflavins. To counteract hot flushes, women should dress lightly, use a cotton sheet at night and avoid spicy foods, hot drinks, caffeine and alcohol. Women who exercise regularly experience fewer hot flushes.

Women who accept menopause as a natural progression in life are likely to sail through it, claims Dr. Miriam Stoppard in her book entitled *Menopause*. Those who think it is a complicated, mysterious illness, or have a negative attitude towards it, are more likely to suffer symptoms. Remaining positive will help a woman become motivated and see the menopause as a liberating process, and a time of opportunity. Many women start entirely new careers at this stage of their lives.

It is vital also that, if you are menopausal, you communicate to your partner how you are feeling so that he will understand what you are going through. It might be helpful to show him a copy of this chapter.

It is important to note that there are many alternatives to taking HRT which will help you deal with the problems you may encounter during menopause. A proper diet and exercise plan can alleviate menopausal symptoms and also will be beneficial to your general health. Soy bean and wholegrain products and various herbs may help you. The latter should be used only after consultation with your doctor and a herbalist, however. The following may be prescribed for hormonal problems:

**Dong Quai** (Angelica Root)
This is a photo-oestrogen that is used to relieve hot flushes, breast tenderness, sore joints, insomnia and anxiety.

**Ginseng**
Another photo-oestrogen, this is used to stimulate the immune system and normalise blood pressure.

**Black Cohosh**
The root of this herb is used to relieve hot flushes, night sweats, vaginal dryness, irritability, anxiety, headaches and depression.

**Liquorice Root**
This will relieve vaginal dryness and hot flushes.

For information on how to ingest these herbs, contact a herbalist. Therapies for stress and the exercises referred to in Chapter 4 are equally applicable for treating the problems of menopause. In addition, treatments such as homeopathy, acupressure and acupuncture can also bring your body back into balance.

If you are suffering from any of these problems, try to be proactive, not reactive like a Dragon Woman!

# CHAPTER 9

# Stop Breathing Fire and Communicate!

*I like talking to a brick wall; it is the only thing in the world that never contradicts me.*

– Oscar Wilde

People often ask me, 'What is the main reason why people divorce or relationships break down?' If I had to answer in just a few words, I would say, 'Communication, or the lack of it.'

There is no doubt that people's failure to communicate well is the single biggest factor leading to relationship breakdowns. Men and women not only find it difficult to talk to each other, but constantly misread each other's body language. This inevitably leads to arguments or silence, both of which can kill a relationship.

Conversation is the glue that can cement otherwise fluid emotions between a man and a woman. It creates the conditions for understanding so that two individuals with different ideals, backgrounds and experiences can come together in a partnership. Through talking, we add to our knowledge and find approval for what we do. Without it, the world becomes a lonely and sterile place.

*The liberation of language is rooted in the liberation of ourselves.*

– Mary Daley

The problem is that men and women are very different. A great deal has been written about the emotional differences between men and women and their differing approaches to communication. In *Men Are from Mars, Women Are from Venus*, John Gray says that men retreat into their caves when they do not wish to communicate and women should understand this. While I believe that men and women do have emotional differences and approach communication differently, they can be taught to communicate better.

> *Question:*    *What have you got in common with your*
>                  *husband?*
> *Answer:*      *We were both married on the same day.*
>                                      – Anon

If partners persistently argue, however, it will not automatically ruin their relationship. We all know of couples who have been married for thirty, forty or fifty years and argue incessantly, but whose relationship can still be regarded as strong.

However, if they never really talk, but just make the occasional remark about the weather, the husband may wake up to find that his wife has run off with the next-door neighbour in an attempt to inject some excitement into life.

In one case that I know about, a couple had not spoken for fifteen years, except to offer each other a morning cup of tea. They had lost the art of communication and drifted through the years until finally the wife could stand it no longer, and left.

It is dangerous also if your only form of communication is to write notes to each other. It is definitely time to take stock if this is happening in your relationship. I would suggest that you arrange a weekend away – without your notepads – and resolve to talk throughout the entire weekend, beginning by discussing every topical item in the newspaper if necessary!

# Dragons Don't Talk, But Women Do

> *Women speak because they wish to speak, whereas a man speaks only when driven to speak by something outside himself, like, for instance, he can't find any clean socks.*
>
> – Jean Kerr

Many of my male clients ask me why women never seem to stop talking. 'Don't they realise how irritating it is?' they say.

## 1. Recognise Her Need to Talk

Women need to talk in order to:

  a. Think through their day

  b. Resolve problems

  c. Build relationships or friendships.

Women resolve their problems by talking around a subject for hours. They find it difficult to understand why men do not approach problems in the same way.

Men must recognise that refusing to allow women to express themselves will lead to their having feelings of intense frustration. A woman who is not given the chance to talk about what she wants to discuss will believe that her partner does not care about her.

## 2. Be Conscious of Her Need for Your Perspective

Subtle hints are lost on men. Women must learn to say what they mean – without being hurtful, of course.

If you want to talk something over aloud, to help you make up your mind, make this clear. There's no point asking your partner to make a choice for you and then berating him when he does. Do not say: 'Should I wear the black or the blue dress?' and, when he says, 'The blue one,' ask: 'What's wrong with the black one?' This will make him want to explode. Instead, tell him: 'I want you to tell me I look great in both. Just listen while I mull it over. I find it really helpful when you join me in this process!' That way, you will both end up laughing and your evening out will be fun instead of degenerating into a battle between the sexes.

## Strong Silent Men Can Talk

*Most men act so tough and strong on the outside
because on the inside we are scared, weak and fragile.
Men, not women, are the weaker sex.*

– Jerry Rubin (1994)

Women cannot understand how men can go fishing, play golf, visit the pub, watch football, etc., with their friends and say literally not a meaningful word for hours. 'How can he be a friend,' a woman may ask her partner, 'if you never really *talk* to him? Did he have any news? How is his marriage? How is his job? What films has he seen? Where is he going on holiday?' All of these tend to interest women, but not men. A man will happily spend time with a male friend and feel totally relaxed in his company without ever feeling the need to discuss such things. Eighty per cent of my male clients never discuss their divorces with any of their men friends, and none of their friends raise their own marital problems with them. They are more likely to talk about them to a female colleague at work.

Men find it extremely difficult to talk about emotional issues, as we have seen. From an early age, girls are conditioned to express their emotions, and boys to suppress them. This is why the majority of men find it so hard to talk about emotional issues.

## 1. Men's Fears

According to my survey results, conversations most feared by divorcing husbands are ones which their wives begin with:

1. 'Let's talk.'
2. 'What are you thinking about?'
3. 'What is troubling you?'
4. 'Is there a problem at work?'
5. 'I don't think you love me.'
6. 'You don't care about me.'
7. 'Do you still fancy me?'
8. 'Why don't we talk any more?'
9. 'What do you really feel about me?'
10. 'Why are you so distant?'

The women interviewed said that the most likely responses from men to the above are:

1. Anger.
2. To change the subject.
3. 'Let's talk about it later.'
4. To walk away, or even leave the house.
5. To 'argue his way out of it' in order to retain control of the situation.

Men feel extremely threatened when women question them like this. They don't understand what they're getting at, and often feel they are being criticised. This makes them more likely to switch off.

**CASE STUDY** ● ● ● ● ● ● ● ● ● ● ● ● ● ●

> Anthony was a doctor. He was highly respected, and extremely articulate when discussing patients and practice administration, for example. At home, he did not

talk much. He was shy and introverted in his personal life. When he was a child, his parents actively discouraged him from sharing his emotions. If he was hurt or upset by anything, he was taught to deal with his distress internally.

Anthony met and married Audrey, a psychologist. Audrey came from a very warm and loving background where things were freely discussed by all the family. This had encouraged her to become a psychologist. She liked people to open up, but Anthony wouldn't. After two years of marriage, this became a source of conflict. Audrey kept asking Anthony questions like: 'You don't really love me, do you?' Anthony, who worked very long hours, would dread these questions. He saw them as darts aimed at him quite needlessly. He would often retort: 'I am not one of your patients. Save your analysis for them.' These answers infuriated Audrey. She just wanted to talk, to be heard, but in her frustration she had abandoned all the skills she had been taught as a psychologist. The more she pushed, the more Anthony shut her off and became aggressive and angry towards her.

One day, Audrey tried a different approach. She asked him a question and tried to explain why she wanted an answer. At last, he started to talk. But, no sooner had he begun – 'I feel very pressured when you ask me about these emotional issues . . .' – than Audrey jumped in, saying, 'Well, I think that is because of your home circumstances.' She was too Dragon Woman-like for Anthony, who clammed up entirely and would not open up again.

The situation deteriorated and eventually they were divorced. Anthony explained, 'It was true that my background caused me difficulties in expressing emotions. I felt constantly under attack.'

Anthony later met Jackie, who did not ask any probing questions. She made him feel safe, and after a few months he was able to open up to her about how he felt. He and Jackie are still in a happy, loving relationship.

* * * * * * * * * * * * * * * * * * * * * *

## 2. Make Him Comfortable

Many men talk to their mistresses about work, relationships and a multitude of subjects that they simply cannot discuss with their wives. The very reason why a man starts an affair is often that the woman with whom he becomes involved is sympathetic and obviously full of admiration for him. This makes him feel safe and in control. He feels that he can speak to her without fear of rejection or criticism. However, once his mistress becomes his wife, their long and interesting conversations will almost certainly cease, and the shutters will come down over him whenever she raises the issue of emotions.

Men will talk only when they feel free from responsibility and safe from criticism. Women will find that men react much more positively if they schedule a sensible time to discuss a problem, with the intention of reaching a positive solution.

Remember that timing is all-important. A woman should never launch into an important conversation when her partner has just come home from work, or when he is just about to go to sleep.

*The first breath of adultery is the freest,*
*after it, constraints aping marriage develop.*
                                                    – John Updike

## How to Get Men to Talk

Having talked to many men in failing relationships, I have realised that such men are quite lonely. They **do** want to talk, but they do not feel safe talking to their partners. This does not make them wimps. It means that, having been conditioned for so long to suppress their emotions, and to direct their energies towards solving problems and reaching solutions instead, they need women to understand them and to create an environment in which they can relax and express themselves freely.

> *To get a man's attention, just stand in front of the TV and don't move. He will talk to you, I promise.*
>
> – Tim Allen

Men complain that women have an infuriating habit of finishing their sentences for them and thus misinterpreting what they are trying to say whenever they do begin to open up a little. While it is a fact that, statistically, men are more likely to interrupt women, if a woman interrupts a man, particularly when they are discussing emotional issues, her partner will be reluctant to expose his feelings again.

## 1. Approach Him Gently

If you so want to encourage your partner to talk, you must avoid sounding critical of him. Explain that you want to talk to him about something that is worrying you; you believe that you may have found a solution, but would like his input. Tell him that, as a woman, it may take you longer than him to reach a conclusion, but talking about it makes you feel better. This should produce a positive reaction. You can then discuss the matter as a couple, and consider 'what *we* want to do about the situation'. It will help to bring you closer together if you discuss problems as partners rather than individuals.

> *To be happy with a man, you must understand him a lot and love him a little. To be happy with a woman, you must love her a lot and not try to understand her at all.*
>
> – Helen Roland

The question 'What are you thinking about?' from a woman to a man will always be met by the answer 'Nothing'. Most women, not content to let the matter rest there, will then say something like: 'Well, you look like something is wrong.' I know this from personal experience. My husband and sons will insist that 'Nothing is wrong,' then add: 'Why are you criticising me?' It wasn't until my family decided to try the same tactics on me every night for a week that I realised how irritating, unhelpful and provocative such remarks can be.

Statements such as: 'It's been a heavy day. What's it been like for you?' or 'Let's have some fun tonight. Life can sometimes be so stressful,' are more likely to unlock your partner's emotions. You do not need to actually go out; the mere suggestion of a pleasant, peaceful evening – a complete contrast to the stressful day he has had at work – is a good opening gambit that should lead to a relaxed and constructive conversation.

*Women like silent men; they think they are listening.*
– Marcell Archard (1956)

## 2. Be Conscious of Your Body Language

Body language can make all the difference to whether a conversation continues or ends. If, when your partner starts to open up, you stand facing him, hands on hips in a threatening stance, he will probably stop talking and walk out of the room. Sitting with your arms and legs tightly crossed gives him the clear message: 'I disagree with you' – and propping up your chin with your hand tells him: 'I am bored with this conversation'. These postures will infuriate him. If you are standing up, do not put your hands on your hips. If you are sitting, try not to cross your arms. Leaving hands and arms open and relaxed indicates that you welcome his approach.

In the divorces I have handled, many husbands have commented that their wives' rigid posture and angry expression during their discussions told them they had no desire to carry on conversations with them.

In his book, *Body Language: How to Read Others' Thoughts by Their Gestures*, Allan Pease suggests that, in any conversation, 35 per cent of communication is verbal and 65 per cent is non-verbal. So if your partner asks if you are listening, for example, it's no good saying 'Yes' when your body language is screaming that you're bored.

Dr. John Gottman, a psychologist, has found that the way in which people communicate can affect their marriages. He claims that a marriage where the wife makes sour facial expressions when her husband talks is likely to end within four years. This seems over-pessimistic. Obviously, when partners are constantly arguing and trying to destroy each other's confidence on a daily basis, it can lead to the rapid demise of a relationship. I do not believe that negative facial expressions and body language alone can predict such an outcome, although it seems sensible that they should be avoided.

## Do Dragons Listen?

Men going through a divorce frequently complain that their wives don't listen to them or hear what they have to say. This may seem strange, given that so many wives say that they can't get their husbands or partners to talk. The fact is that today's Dragon Women are so intent on putting forward their own views that they have forgotten the most important part of communication: **Listening**. A conversation should be a non-threatening, two-way process, where neither partner feels in competition with the other.

*The reason why so few people are agreeable in
conversation is that each is thinking more about what
he intends to say than about what others are saying,
and we never listen when we are eager to speak.*

– Francois Duc de la Rochefoucauld (1665)

**CASE STUDY** ● ● ● ● ● ● ● ● ● ● ● ● ● ● ● ●

Robert was easygoing, Rachel much more pushy. When
she went to work, she became very bossy and Dragon-
like. She believed that she was right about most things.

Robert began to have problems at work. Rachel
noticed he looked worried, and kept asking him, 'What's
the matter with you?' He always replied, 'Nothing'. Rachel
would nag him to tell her what was wrong and why he
was so distant. Her manner was so aggressive that he
just couldn't find the words to talk to her, although he
longed to discuss his problems. Rachel made him feel as
if he was standing in front of the school headmistress,
and he simply couldn't open up.

The situation worsened, and Robert and Rachel went
into therapy. Robert told the therapist about his inability
to communicate with Rachel. The therapist asked him:
'Do you feel that Rachel cares about you?' 'Yes, I do,' he
replied. The therapist then asked in what circumstances
Robert would be able to talk to his wife about his
problems. 'If Rachel would stop being so threatening and
accusing, I would love to talk to her,' he answered. Rachel
learned to adopt an open posture when she spoke with
Robert and to say things like, 'I've had a rotten day. You
look as though you may have, too. It can be awful when
work is so stressful. I would love to talk to you about it
for about half an hour. How about you?' When they
practised this in therapy, Robert said that this approach
was helpful to him; it gave him 'the green light to offload'. Rachel listened attentively, without interrupting,
and allowed him to finish. At the end, she gave him a
big hug.

Since that time, Rachel and Robert have communicated well. When they have something to discuss, neither will interrupt or be judgmental, and each will offer a potential solution, which they talk about together without shouting. They communicate as equals, considering each other's views with respect. 'Solving problems should be a team effort,' they say.

\* \* \* \* \* \* \* \* \* \* \* \* \* \* \* \* \* \* \* \* \* \*

Communication isn't always easy, but if you can respect your partner's opinions, and make it safe for them to be expressed, you are more likely to arrive at decisions jointly as a couple. When you do, your relationship will prosper, and you will be the happier for it.

*Remember, people will not respond positively to you unless you respond positively to them.*

– Anon

# CHAPTER 10

# Coping with Men's Behaviour

*Basically my wife was immature: I'd be at home in the bath and she would come in and sink my boats.*

– Woody Allen

Many Dragon Women say that men are boys who have just aged and don't want to grow up or take responsibility. While this may be true of some men, fortunately not all are like this. Most of those who are like little boys have been spoilt by their mothers and expect similar treatment from their wives.

*Once I went out with this guy who asked me to mother him. I spat on his hanky and wiped his face.*

– Jenny Jones

Wives who collude with them thus get what they themselves continue to create: a man who can do nothing for himself. So if you mother him as his mother did before you, you have no right to complain about what you produce.

You should, however, be aware that, if you mother him, he may begin to see you as a mother figure and rebel, either by not helping you like a naughty child or by running away. It is your responsibility to break the pattern or put up with it.

> *Man = A domestic animal, which, if treated with*
> *firmness and kindness, can be trained in most things.*
>
> — Jilly Cooper

Probably his mother always picked up after him when he was a child, so he never learned the skill of doing this for himself. A woman might say, 'Well so did my mother, but it hasn't stopped me. I clear up now, so why can't he?'

The answer is that women adapt to the mother role, but men do not. If boys are not taught to clean up after themselves, they will not bother to do so as men unless reprogrammed.

> *A man's home may seem to be his castle from the*
> *outside: inside, it is more often his nursery.*
>
> — Clare Boothe-Luce

## How to Reprogramme a Man

At risk of sounding as if I am advocating Dragon Woman behaviour in the home, after all of my admonitions against it, following are suggestions for handling common problems, but *without* Dragon Woman behaviour, which women who find themselves in a Peter Pan syndrome may find helpful.

1. **Why does he always throw his clothes on the floor and expect me to pick them up?**

   If you cannot abide clothes or mess being left around your home, your first reaction as a woman is to clear them away. *Don't*. While it will be extremely difficult for you to do this, and your temptation to give in will be overwhelming, you must hold firm. Let the washing pile up until he does not have one clean shirt, pair of socks or underwear. He will soon catch on. You must, however, advise him in a soft voice that you would be most grateful if he could pick up his things and put

them in the laundry bin or hang them up. If you keep
repeating this in a non-judgmental manner, he will
learn, like the dog in Pavlov's experiment, that if he does
this, he will receive a reward. You must give him your
approval when he tells you with child-like satisfaction
that he has now put the laundry in the bin and carried
it downstairs, or else he will revert to his old ways. Do
not throw the washing out of the window. This will not
help. You will merely make him think you are a Dragon
Woman.

*Most men do not do laundry because washers don't
come with remote control.*

– TV Advertisement

2. **Why does he expect me to run his bath or wash his
   hair?**
   If you both enjoy doing this, then there is no reason for
   you to stop, but if it annoys you, then do stop doing it.
   The next time he asks you for assistance, say, 'I'm busy
   right now.' He will soon get the message.

*Question: Why is psychoanalysis so much quicker for
men than for women?*
*Answer: Because when it is time to go back to his
childhood, he is already there.*

– Helen Rowland

3. **Why doesn't he ever ask for directions and I always
   have to find the right way to go?**
   Most men will not ask for directions because of their
   inherent hunting instincts and belief that they can find
   their own way. However, if you are always the one he
   depends on to point out that he has just missed the
   turning or motorway exit, he will never learn. Do not tell

him. Sit there and let him learn from his mistakes, even
if he becomes very angry with you. Leave a map inside
the car door, or, if he drives you to insanity, consider
buying him a Routemaster or a satellite navigation
system so that he can programme his routes without
losing face. Do remember, however, that telling a man he
can't find something is an attack on his manhood which
should be avoided at all costs.

4. **Why can't he ever find his own keys or his wallet and
   why does he seem to blame me when he loses them?**
   This must be a man's most irritating habit. It is not the
   mislaying of anything that is annoying, but the
   accusatory way in which he says, 'Where have you put
   my keys?' Your retort, 'Where have I put your keys? You
   mean where have you mislaid them! Why can't you ever
   accept the blame for anything? Why is it always me?',
   will lead to a flaming row. So do not respond this way
   or argue; just let him find things for himself. Eventually
   he will see that he must go it alone or be more careful in
   future. However, you might install a key rack at home
   so that it will become second nature for him to hang
   them up, or, if you're worried about burglars, set up a
   key box to which you hold the key. As for the wallet, for
   his next birthday, buy him a wallet box to keep beside
   the bed.

5. **Why does he have the same meal for twenty times
   and love it, and then say that he doesn't like it when I
   make it for him on the 21st occasion?**
   It is one of life's mysteries why a man will love a
   particular meal that is prepared on endless occasions
   and then abruptly decide he dislikes it. Perhaps it has
   taken a long time for him to admit he dislikes it, his
   tastebuds have changed or he has become bored with

the familiar. Sometimes, though, a man behaves like a naughty child about a meal. If this happens, I suggest:

• Do not throw it all over him.

• Do not fall into a mood.

• Don't scream, 'But you love it!'

• Don't feed it to the dog.

• Do avoid making it again.

• Ask that he tells you what meal he prefers so that you will not feel put out.

• If he persists with this behaviour about everything you make, stop cooking for him!

6. **Why won't he ever help around the house, making any excuse to delay even the simplest of household chores?**

It is precisely because you and his mother have always responded to his every whim that he will not help around the house. (A study carried out in 2000 by a Cambridge graduate showed that, in general, women do 35 hours of housework a week. Men contribute a maximum of five.) Leave the Hoover in front of the television and say to him in a soft voice, 'I would really appreciate it if you could help me with the hoovering.' It is likely that he will not do anything until he has been asked several times. Do not get angry; do not start a row; do not switch off the television.

Men respond to gentle persuasion, not coercion. Sometimes even a hint of a later reward will galvanise him into action.

If he does help with the housework or hoovering, praise him. Do not show him that he hasn't carried out a particular task properly; the more he does it, the more skilled he will become.

If, despite your protests, he won't help, wait until he settles down to read the newspaper and then quietly ask: 'Have you got [the handyman's] number so I can ask him to put up the shelves? I know you have a lot to do.' Once this filters through, he will most certainly jump into action and say, 'No, I will do it!' Give him a few hours and then repeat the question.

If he still does not respond, then make the call. Smile sweetly as you do it, with no obvious anger or aggression, and you are more likely to get your way.

However, if you telephone the handyman without giving him a chance to do the job, he will be only too delighted and will never learn to do things himself.

*Question: What does the word 'macho' stand for?*
*Answer: Men Avoiding Chores at Home and Outside.*

– Anon

# Handling Irritating Habits

Many women tell me that they do not have irritating habits themselves, while their partners have so many. It is true that men are generally more easy-going and don't notice many things that women do. However, things that will irritate a man include: a woman using his razor (this will send him into orbit), plucking hairs from her face, using hair remover cream and breaking wind.

For women, the proverbial straw that can break the camel's back of a relationship is a man's habit of zapping the remote controller on the television. During 1999, this was the most frequent complaint I heard from women. At the end of a hard day, many women want to unwind by becoming involved in a television programme or watching advertisements. Men will zap through adverts and programmes as their method of unwinding. Many men are not even conscious that this is what they are doing. Men cannot understand, having reached Channel 129, why their wives have stormed out of the room. A woman believes, if a man zaps without regard for what might interest her, that he is selfish, bored, doesn't care about and no longer loves her, and will likely go off with someone else. Men have no idea that zapping can cause such a reaction. Even if they do, they will probably continue to zap! They love gadgets and playing with them, and find it relaxing to do so.

In an ideal world, men should be reprogrammed to understand that this is annoying. One way a woman may do this is to walk out of the room when he zaps and watch another television. If he wants you to be with him, he will ask why you have gone. Explain in a calm way that you cannot watch television when he zaps and that it gives you a migraine, but will be happy to watch with him when he stops changing channels. Alternatively, buy another remote control to zap the television yourself, until he stops – or take up a hobby like reading.

There are no easy answers to zapping. You can perhaps try showing this chapter to your partner, explaining how miserable his actions have made you and the rest of the family, and how you would love him to stop. While I do not recommend rewarding bad behaviour, if all else fails, try hinting that if he stops zapping, he will be suitably rewarded. This usually works and you may find that you will watch far less television as a result.

**CASE STUDY** ●●●●●●●●●●●●●●●

> Gloria always felt that she was a rational woman. She looked after her family and held down a reasonable part-time job, but if there was one thing that she could not cope with, it was Derek's remote control zapping of the television.

Night after night, Derek would zap through the channels so that, no sooner had Gloria seen something that looked interesting, they were twenty stations on. At first she tried to deal with it by asking, 'Derek, must you do that?'

He would reply, 'Do what?'

'You know, zap though the channels.'

'Oh,' he would say and continue.

One day, Gloria had been looking forward to watching the second part of a three-part series that was due to be broadcast at 9 o'clock. At three minutes to nine, Derek started to zap. She asked Derek if he could please remember that her programme started at 9.00. As if hypnotised, Derek barely replied. He was zapping up and down the channels with fervour. Gloria sat grinding her teeth until her watch showed 9.05.

She later described how she calmly walked over to a side table, picked up an ashtray and threw it through the screen. Derek was horrified and watched the television screen disintegrate. He told her that she was insane and needed help. Gloria replied, 'Urghhh,' and walked out of the room.

When Derek subsequently sought advice from a solicitor about injunction proceedings, saying that he did not wish to become divorced, but wished to stop Gloria from destroying any more television sets, he described his wife's behaviour as unreasonable. His lawyer explained that actually *she* could quite understand why Gloria had done it, and suggested that Derek ought to think about therapy for them both, which they both underwent. Derek has never zapped again and they have both taken up gardening.

＊＊＊＊＊＊＊＊＊＊＊＊＊＊＊＊＊＊＊＊＊

Question:    *How do you get a man to exercise?*
Answer:      *Put a remote control between his feet.*

— Anon

# Understanding Sports Obsessions

Girls play with dolls; boys play with balls. As adults, women have children to replace dolls; men still play with balls!

Many women cannot understand men's attachment to sport. Women believe that, because they are ready to give up their hobbies for men, men should do the same for them.

In our changing world where men's jobs are under threat, and they understand women less and less, there are only a few things in life which men find secure, unchanging and certain. One of them is sport. Men fantasise that they are making the plays that their heroes are. When a man sees his team win, it exhilarates him. Feeling part of a group makes him feel strong. The more confusing men find this world, the more they cling to sport – a sphere where they are not criticised and efforts are not being made to change them, where they are accepted for who they are. This is why they will spend money on a season ticket instead of a new sofa, or a new set of golf clubs instead of a holiday. Being successful on the golf course or in a game of tennis gives men self-esteem which has been lost in the workplace or at home.

A woman married to a man like this is called a football or golf widow. This means she is left alone while he pursues his hobby.

I have been involved in many cases where sport has been the factor which made women decide to end their relationship. Particularly at the time of the World Cup, many women complain that it is as if their husbands press the minimise button on their lives, taking them to a box at the bottom of their computers where they stay until the season is over. For such a problem, you may wish to consider the following:

a. If your relationship is worth waiting until the end of the season for, compromise and agree that, when the team is not playing, he spend time with you and the children, then mark dates in your diary for spending special days together.

b. While he plays his sport, take up a new hobby or get together with other wives.

c. You could try joining in. Ask if you can come to some of the matches. Many women find that, once they understand and experience the atmosphere, they become as caught up in it as their partners.

d. You can watch lots of 'girlie movies' that he would never watch with you.

e. You can make him promise to watch Wimbledon with you every day in return for watching football on television with him.

f. You can go shopping. (In time, he may find it cheaper to go out with you rather than to watch football.)

> *If we did get a divorce, the only way he would know it is if they announced it on Wide World of Sports.*
>
> – Dr. Joyce Brothers

**CASE STUDY** * * * * * * * * * * * * * * *

Judy would sulk every time Malcolm went to a football match. After he returned, she would slam things around in the kitchen and be most unpleasant. She felt very lonely and abandoned while he was away. Malcolm began to dread her moods, but was not prepared to give up his sport. Eventually, Malcolm asked Judy if she would go with him to a match; grumpily, she agreed. Once there, Judy became so enthralled that she began shouting and felt completely exhilarated. Judy now wears her own sports gear and arranges for all of her friends to accompany her and Malcolm to games. She has never been closer to Malcolm.

* * * * * * * * * * * * * * * * * * * *

# Coping with Competing Careers

> *I would be willing to bet that if one day a woman*
> *walked barefoot to the moon and back and a man*
> *cleaned out his desk, when the two of them sat down*
> *to dinner that night he would say, 'Boy was that desk*
> *a mess.'*
>
> – Margot Kaufman

'Why is it that men expect you to build up their careers by entertaining or going to their business dinners with enthusiasm,' ask some women, 'but are not willing to do the same for you?'

Many women claim that some men are very jealous of women's success. If other people comment upon the success of such a man's wife, he will often say something like, 'Give me a bucket – ooh aren't you famous – or you are so famous now you won't want to cook for little old me anymore!'

What women don't always understand is that men in this situation do not have the skills to deal with their partner's success. They feel very threatened. They believe that when a woman becomes successful, she will not respect their views anymore, or not find them attractive, and may find someone else and leave them. Because many men are unable to express their insecurities, they become angry and unnecessarily lash out or show a propensity for insulting her at every opportunity.

If you are in this situation, there is no point shouting at or berating him. It will get you nowhere. You must give him the reassurance he needs and tell him that your success is for him to share with you. Remember to praise him and ask for his advice, listening attentively when he gives it to you.

Regrettably, Dragon Women have become so arrogant and critical of their partners, that when they do become successful, they often drive them into the arms of another woman who makes them feel needed and appreciated. The key to avoiding this is assuaging his fears with an abundance of attention and reassurance. The solution is not to simply tell him to grow up, as so many Dragon Women do.

Many women also complain that men do not want to hear about their work problems. As I mentioned in Chapter 9, the solution is do not keep bombarding him with your endless work problems – he will not be able to relax; set a timetable for discussions with him and stick to it.

**CASE STUDY** ● ● ● ● ● ● ● ● ● ● ● ● ● ● ●

> When they first met, Katy was an up and coming television actress, and Tim was a moderately successful actor. As Katy's career took off, she noticed that when the phone rang for her with television offers, Tim would become surly and turn up the sound on the television or tell her to hurry up. When they went out to parties or restaurants, if anyone remarked upon her performances, he would turn away and seem resentful. He would regularly find fault with everything she did at home or tell her that she looked washed out.
>
> Katy didn't have the resources to deal with him. She was tired from her success and exhausted from the emotional stress caused by Tim. Eventually, she could take no more and left him.
>
> If Tim had understood his own insecurities, he would have been able to give Katy more encouragement and not attempted to destroy her confidence. If Katy hadn't been so insecure, she would have understood how her success had made Tim insecure and then could have dealt with it.

● ● ● ● ● ● ● ● ● ● ● ● ● ● ● ● ● ● ● ● ● ● ●

Where an insecure ego meets another insecure ego, there is likely to be a power struggle. In most cases, they will both lose.

# Avoid Criticising Him and Let Him Take the Credit

> *Women will sometimes admit to making mistakes.*
> *The last man who admitted that he was wrong was*
> *General George Custer.*
>
> – Matt Groening

There is a fundamental universal rule which applies to all men: they do not like criticism. They find it very difficult to accept that their approach to a situation or crisis is incorrect because inherent in most men is a need to solve difficult situations successfully. This is what men believe they should do. When his partner is always right, and he is wrong, a man will lose his self-esteem and wish to be with someone who makes him feel strong again.

**CASE STUDY** ● ● ● ● ● ● ● ● ● ● ● ● ● ●

Stuart was not a good driver. Sylvia was constantly telling him that he was tailgating someone, going too fast or too slow, or driving too near parked cars. Stuart would jerk the car as he drove because Sylvia made him so nervous.

On one occasion, Sylvia spent a long journey telling him what an awful driver he was. Upon their return home, Sylvia got out of the car and went into the house – only to hear a bang. Stuart, in an angry state due to Sylvia, had driven into the dustbin beside their fence, which duly crashed over. Sylvia ran outdoors, crying, 'What have you done?'

Stuart retorted, 'I haven't done anything.'

Sylvia, who began divorce proceedings shortly afterwards, felt that he was completely hopeless and would never admit he was wrong. She said he kept telling her that she had caused the accident.

● ● ● ● ● ● ● ● ● ● ● ● ● ● ● ● ● ● ● ●

The reason why a man says he is not to blame for something is because, in his mind, if a woman is critical of him and he does something wrong, he attributes the blame to her criticism of him. To a man, this is perfectly logical. To a woman, it is childish.

> *In passing, I would like to say that the first time*
> *Adam had a chance, he laid the blame on women.*
>
> – Lady Nancy Astor

So avoid criticising him too much. If he does something wrong, do not gloat, but don't accept the full blame either. A calm approach, without suggesting that you help, is the best way forward. If he wants your help, he will ask for it. While your offer is well intentioned, he will interpret it as you gloating over his discomfort.

Similarly, men like to take the credit for getting things right. If you are enjoying a holiday, a man will tell you that it was his idea. This can be infuriating to the woman whose idea it was. The sensible way forward is not to make a fuss, or say, 'But you didn't even want to come on this holiday.' Pointing out his mistake will not improve your relationship. The www.woman will let him think it was his idea. Since you are enjoying yourself anyway, is there any need to spoil the moment?

> *Man likes his wife to be just clever enough to*
> *comprehend his cleverness and just stupid enough to*
> *admire it.*
>
> – Israel Zangwill

# Men's Impatience with Shopping

Surveys carried out in 1999 demonstrated scientifically that men do not like to go food or clothes shopping. They feel threatened in the environment of a shopping centre and become very bored and frustrated. Those who stay the course tend to take a very domineering attitude with the trolley, determined to conduct the exercise in a way they choose to structure it.

Most men will drive trolleys straight up and down aisles as they shop, whereas most women move in a zigzag pattern. Either way, each tends to irritate the other by their different driving habits. My suggestion is to let him drive the trolley, because men like to feel in control, and, if necessary, zigzag across the aisle yourself.

If you insist on taking him clothes shopping, expect him to adopt an air of hopelessness after half an hour, especially if you ask him which outfit he prefers. Try not to expose him to this no-win question and don't expect him to understand why you must try on 100 outfits to his two. A man is much more direct in his shopping habits. He can go into a shop and choose three suits and four shirts in ten minutes. A woman can take all afternoon to decide on one blouse. Do not expect him to understand this.

To avoid problems with him:

a. Don't shop with him unless he enjoys it.

b. If you must go food shopping together, try to make it fun. Ask him occasionally what he would like rather than talking about what food you should buy for the dog.

c. If you are spending a lot of money, don't expect him to be as thrilled about it as you; if he is doing the buying, show him that you are really grateful.

d. If you are spending money buying clothes, show some interest in him by buying something for him as well as yourself. Tell him how handsome he looks in something that suits him, and he won't mind what shopping you do after that.

# Family Problems

The worst rows that couples have usually concern family matters. These occur most frequently over the Christmas period, which is why, statistically, the end of December and beginning of January is the peak time for divorces. Such rows usually involve the following.

## 1. Criticising your partner's mother or father

Never ever criticise your partner's parents unless you are invited by your partner to do so. For instance, there can be many underlying problems between mothers and daughters-in-law which involve a struggle for power over a man. This is particularly noticeable when a mother who has always done everything for her son finds it difficult to let him go. Never expect a man to choose between his family and you. If you do not put him in that position, neither of you will have to face difficult choices.

If your mother-in-law is trying to interfere in your relationship, it is unlikely that your husband will see this. Men are often oblivious to power play between women, essentially because they are generally visual and not verbal so do not notice subtle nuances which a woman's radar picks up immediately. Your best way of dealing with a mother-in-law problem is by dealing directly with her, not her son. Either demonstrate where the power lies so that she will stop intruding, or try to talk to her in order to allay her fears of exclusion, then include her as much as possible in your family.

## 2. Accusing your partner of wanting to spend more time with his family than yourself

Make sure that you occasionally allow your partner private time to spend with parents, siblings or children from a previous marriage. You will be surprised how grateful your partner will be for your understanding when you allow this without feeling resentful.

## 3. Buying better gifts for one's own family than that of one's partner

Try to be sensitive about buying gifts for both of your families. Spend the same amount for both. Your partner will be grateful for your efforts.

## 4. Someone listening more to their own family than their partner

Do accommodate suggestions which come from members of your partner's family. Listen and consider them before rejecting them out-of-hand, or you may miss a good idea.

# How to Keep Your Day Off for Yourself

When a woman says that she is having a day off, a man instinctively wants to fill it up for her. He will make endless lists of tasks for you to undertake on your day off. This is because he is afraid that you will find that you prefer to spend your time elsewhere, away from him.

The solution to this problem is to try to do some, but not all, of the tasks. Tell him that you tried your best, but there just wasn't sufficient time in the day. If you keep repeating this, he will soon get the message and stop asking.

Men believe that their work is more important than women's. This is because, until recently, men were intended to be the breadwinners and women the nurturers in our society. While things may have changed, most men have not.

# Changing Childish Men

Most women love helpless men and instinctively try to mother them, but this can become a nightmare when you have to live with them. So women often try to mould men into what they would like them to be: from unsuccessful to successful, quiet to talkative, weak to strong. Quite often, they will end up with a distortion of their ideal and decide that they do not like him now that he has changed. To women I would say, if you do what Dr. Frankenstein did, you may end up with a mutation who might turn on you. If you nag at a weak man to become strong, he will develop qualities which will give him the strength to leave you just to get away from your constant criticism. If you want your partner to change for the better, encourage, praise and gently persuade him. Then he will want to change so that he can have a partnership rather than a power struggle with you.

> *Why does a woman work for ten years to change a man's habits and then complain that he is not the man she married?*
>
> – Barbra Streisand

Men can be very childish, but if women were to eliminate all of their less admirable traits, the world would no doubt become a very boring and unhappy place. In any case, they will run from a Dragon Woman who tries too hard to change them.

> *The only time a woman really succeeds in changing a man is when he is a baby.*
>
> – Natalie Wood

# CHAPTER 11

# Escape from the Dragon's Den

*The honeymoon is the period when the bride still trusts the groom's word of honour.*

– Anon

We all know adultery exists, but do we truly understand what it is? The answer is a firm no. I have been amazed at the number of people who have claimed that their partner has committed adultery, only to find that either their partner has merely kissed someone else, held their hand, cuddled them, flirted with them or even simply been given a lift in their car! For the record, none of these ranks as adultery.

The legal definition of adultery, for which a divorce petition can be issued, is sexual intercourse. Penetration, however slight, must have taken place. We are not talking about the Clinton kind of intercourse, but sexual intercourse in the normal sense. Oral sex is not adultery; it can be regarded (in Britain) as unreasonable behaviour or (in America) as inappropriate liaison. Oral sex is not, nor can it ever be, adultery.

So, in legal terms, what is the difference between an affair and adultery? The answer is absolutely nothing, except that we understand adultery to include a single incident of sexual infidelity with no emotional attachment or significance, whereas an affair is adultery which continues beyond a single occasion.

Adultery figures feature in abundance in my caseload. Men commit adultery with women and women with men. In recent years, there have, of course, been cases questioning whether intercourse between two men or between two women can be considered adultery. Interestingly, while this may be regarded as unreasonable behaviour, and therefore grounds for divorce, it cannot be classified as adultery.

Having therefore cleared up any mystery about the technicalities, I will now move on to deal with the emotional issues.

> *I know many married men, I even know a few happily married men, but I don't know one who wouldn't fall down the first open coal hole running after the first pretty girl who gave him a wink.*
>
> – George Jean Nathan

Over the years, I have acted for many husbands who have had affairs and/or committed adultery, and one conclusion stands out in big, bold letters: **Men can and do have one-off sexual experiences that do not even begin to impact on their psyche**. In other words, although physically it may be an intensely erotic experience, to them it is no more than a release of sexual tension, without any emotional significance whatsoever. One adulterous husband described this sort of sex as being 'as functional as going to the lavatory, with the same sense of release; once done, immediately forgotten'. Another likened his sexual urge to 'a cow that needed milking'.

To most women, this is incomprehensible. This is because men and women have entirely different attitudes to sex, its importance in a relationship and the concept of monogamy.

I believe it is vital that women begin to understand these differences, because it could save so many relationships that would otherwise be destroyed by their reaction to adultery.

> *I wouldn't trust my husband with a young woman for five minutes, and he has been dead for 25 years.*
> – Mrs. Brendan Behan

Women might ask, 'Surely you should be telling men not to commit adultery? If they didn't, the problem would not exist!' This is a little naive. A vast body of research into this area proves that men were created with an inherent urge to procreate, or 'spread their seed'. Recent research shows differences between the brain patterns of men and women, which demonstrate that men are attracted to women visually.

The naked truth is that women are fighting against basic biological facts when they insist that men should remain forever monogamous. They may argue: 'How is it, then, that many men love just one partner and remain faithful to her? Does that mean there is something unnatural about them?' No! It means that civilised man has, over thousands of years, in certain circumstances, learned to curb his natural instincts. (This is not true of all men, of course!)

> *The charm of marriage is that it makes a life of deception absolutely necessary for both parties.*
> – Oscar Wilde

## Why Do People Have Affairs?

During my years as a lawyer, men and women have given me all sorts of answers to the question 'Why did you have an affair?' In 1999, I carried out a poll of my clients. All those who had had an affair were asked to give their reasons for doing so in order of priority. The results made fascinating reading.

For men, the answers were:

1. Lust.
2. 'My wife began to look like her mother.'
3. 'She not only looked like her mother – she started to talk like her as well.'
4. Absence or reduction of sex after marriage.
5. Persistent claims of tiredness by their partner.
6. Wives or partners nagging.
7. Women threw themselves at them.
8. Lack of effort on the part of their partners.
9. The allure of the lack of responsibility associated with an affair.
10. Lack of communication with their wives or partners.

> *Definition of a husband: someone who is chiefly a good lover when he is betraying his wife.*
>
> – Marilyn Monroe

For women, the reasons given were:

1. Boredom.
2. Opportunity.
3. Loneliness.
4. Not being appreciated by their husbands or partners.
5. Lack of interesting sex.
6. Husband's resemblance to Woody Allen (both in appearance and hang-ups).
7. Desire for excitement and romance.
8. Lack of communication.
9. A sense of power when holding down an important job.
10. General desire to escape.

Interestingly, men placed the blame on women – for 'throwing themselves at them' wherever they went. My first reaction, having seen some of these men, was one of surprise, and some disbelief. When I queried this with one client, he told me, 'In the office, they see me as a cross between George Clooney and Mel Gibson.' He said he seemed to 'give off a fascinating aura of power and charm' that wafted up the nostrils of female employees, who were powerless in the face of his magnetism.

> *One man's folly is another man's wife.*
> – Helen Roland

Some men blamed women for encouraging them into illicit liaisons by exercising what they referred to as 'the art of subtle seduction'. I cannot agree with this. No subtlety was needed as far as the majority of the men interviewed were concerned.

> *The happiness of a married man depends on the woman to whom he is not married.*
> – Oscar Wilde

Some men claimed that they were better husbands for having had affairs. Similarly, some women said that after their lovers had taken them to exotic places, they would come home and make wonderful meals for their husbands, and be very attentive to them.

A survey carried out by Relate, the marriage-guidance counsellors, found that one fifth of those having affairs reported that it had improved their existing relationship. This is all well and good if the affair is kept casual. When it becomes more serious, it can and will dangerously affect the marriage or relationship.

# What Statistics Say

The statistics about adultery are fascinating, albeit misleading. In Britain, statisticians use divorce petitions citing adultery to compile their data, but this is a nonsense. As I previously indicated, the divorce petition is only a vehicle to end a marriage and does not reflect the underlying reason for it. The reality is that men who have committed adultery may not admit it, but will ask their wives to petition on the grounds of their unreasonable behaviour. To statisticians, the data will suggest an increase in unreasonable behaviour by men, whereas in fact there has been a marked increase in adultery as a cause for divorce.

From my knowledge of what actually takes place in clients' households, I would estimate that 75 per cent of married men have or will have an affair during the course of their marriage. Of those who have had an affair, 40 per cent will be discovered, either intentionally or otherwise, and 60 per cent will never be found out. Of the 40 per cent whose adultery is discovered, 65 per cent choose to confess to wives, and 35 per cent don't care whether or not they are discovered. Approximately 40 per cent of married women have or will have an affair during the course of their marriage. Of those, only 15 per cent will be found out, and the adultery of 85 per cent will remain undiscovered.

I have compiled these statistics by drawing on records over my 22 years in practice as a divorce lawyer and wide-ranging discussions with men, women, statisticians, Relate marriage counsellors and therapists. I believe that these figures are the most accurate data available on the subject.

# To Confess, or Not to Confess?

By the time they come to seek my advice, many husbands have already chosen to confess their adultery and often seem startled and totally unprepared for their wives' or partners' reaction to their confession. Since the episode meant nothing to him, a husband cannot understand why his wife should not feel exactly the same way about it. He feels that, because he has been so honest, his wife should thank him for his honesty. The attitude many men have to this subject is as naïve, or downright stupid, as the suggestion that men should never have affairs.

> *A husband should tell his wife everything he is sure she will find out, and before anyone else does.*
>
> – Lord Thomas Dewar

A woman believes she should be the most important person in her man's life, because (usually) he is the centre of hers. Most women are conditioned to want to please men and be loved by them. They will do everything they can to obtain love and affection, sometimes sacrificing their own needs to those of the men they love. They therefore expect them to do the same. A woman who is committed to a man in a loving relationship will usually not want to be touched by or to have sex with any other man; the mere thought may be abhorrent to her. She will expect her man to think and feel the same. If he has sex with someone else, she will believe that he prefers the other woman to her. Therefore, he no longer loves her, and her world has fallen apart.

On the whole, women are basically insecure creatures who want constant reassurance. For a woman, adultery equates to the very opposite of reassurance. She is not as sexy, attractive or as sexually adept as the woman her man had sex with. So her husband's confession of adultery may make her explode, particularly if her sense of security has recently been undermined by any other distressing events in the family or at work.

'What?' cries the husband, reeling with shock. 'All that

reaction from one sentence – "I had sex and it meant nothing to me"?'

Yes! Men must understand that, while their adultery meant nothing to them, it will bring to the surface all their partner's negative feelings about themselves.

Controversial as this may seem, I strongly believe that confessions about isolated, casual sexual encounters *should be avoided at all costs*. In this instance, silence *is* golden.

**CASE STUDY** • • • • • • • • • • • • • •

As a salesman, George regularly travelled around the country. After six years with Theresa, he felt that they had a wonderful marriage. The separations seemed to help; they couldn't wait to be alone together as soon as he returned.

On one of his trips, George met Julie in the bar of the hotel where he was staying. They were attracted to each other, and had sex that night. The next morning, George left for another location. He never saw Julie again. However, George felt guilty. He agonised for weeks and months about whether he should tell Theresa what he had done.

Then his mother died. He was in a very low state emotionally. Suddenly struck by the idea that life was too short for secrets, he decided to tell Theresa what had happened with Julie three months earlier.

He said that he was very sorry and he wanted her to know that it meant nothing to him and that he loved her. Theresa did not receive the news well. She packed her bags that night and a week later instigated divorce proceedings.

Theresa's father had left her mother for another woman. For Theresa, George's actions were unforgivable. She did not understand his point of view at all and told him: 'If I had never known, it would have been better, but I *do* know and I can't live with it.' They were divorced.

• • • • • • • • • • • • • • • • • • • • • •

To a man like this, the situation is simple: he had a one-night stand. It was fun, but meant nothing. Now he wants to get it off his chest, he loves his wife and doesn't want to keep things from her. 'After all,' he thinks, 'it was just sex – I don't love the girl. So it can't do any harm to confess.' He has no idea of the storm he's about to unleash.

So why do men frequently want to tell? Having spoken to many such men, I believe they find it cathartic to offload their feelings of guilt.

But men have double standards when the tables are turned. While a man would regard his own infidelities as unimportant, if his wife or partner confessed to a casual sexual encounter, let alone an affair, he would become inconsolable and angry and would never allow it to be forgotten.

To a man, the fact that his partner has let someone else have sex with her (which is how he probably sees it) is not only an assault on his manhood, but on men in general! My advice to a woman who has a one-off sexual experience is the same: do *not* kiss and tell!

> *I say I don't sleep with married men, but what I mean
> is that I don't sleep with happily married men.*
> – Britt Ekland (1980)

Some therapists believe that keeping a guilty secret can seriously affect a relationship and even destroy it. If you feel that your partner can accept your infidelity and believe you when you say that it meant nothing, it might be safe for you to confess. Nevertheless, it is a very bold step – from which there is no return.

Women frequently tell me: 'I kept asking him whether he was having an affair; I nagged him endlessly about it until one day he said: "Yes, I did have a fling. So what? It meant nothing. Are you satisfied now?".' They often add that it was far worse after they knew, because then they were forced to decide whether to stay in their relationship. The fundamental question is, would women rather know if their partners are having an affair? Most women would answer 'Yes', particularly if they find out that their partner has been having a long-term affair. 'If only someone had told me. Everyone seemed to know except me. It is so humiliating,' they cry. However, just as many say that knowing about their husband's adultery has moved the goal-posts and forced a decision they would not otherwise have had to face.

There are no easy answers to this fascinating conundrum. Everyone is different and their reactions to such a confession will vary from one individual to another.

It is interesting, however, that women who have affairs are less likely than men to be found out, for the following reasons:

- Women don't generally confess or see the need to do so.
- Men generally do.
- Women are much more adept at covering their tracks.
- Men leave endless clues.
- Women think with their brains in these situations.
- Men think with a part of their anatomy much further south than their brain when it comes to matters involving sex.
- Women plan their affairs much more carefully than men.
- Men don't plan so much; often it 'just happens'.

> *All men are thieves of love and like a woman all the better for being another's property.*
> – John Gay (1728)

# What Happens Next

Once your partner has confessed to adultery, or you have discovered their infidelity, what is your next step?

Most women say that finding out feels like a serious body blow. Their whole world may seem unreal, as if the man they live with has become a complete stranger, an enemy instead of a friend, someone to suspect instead of trust. It is as though they don't know their partner. It is even worse when an affair has been going on for some time. Wives begin to wonder whether everything their husbands have told them – about their finances, their love for them and their children, their work, friendships, background and family – is a complete lie.

It is important that both parties understand each other's insecurities, so they can work at saving the relationship. Sadly, many couples in this situation do not have the capacity to do this. Their overwhelming feelings of betrayal, rage and mistrust may prevent them from entering into any sensible discussion. They may be quite unable to explain how or why they feel the way they do. Most therapists will agree that the injured party has the right to feel angry and betrayed. If you are in this position, it is important that your partner recognises this right and does not try to convince you that you are wrong to have such feelings. Being angry is normal, but prolonging your anger indefinitely is unreasonable and counter-productive if you want to save your relationship.

Many men believe in the principle of 'forgive and forget': once they have said they are sorry and a suitable period of what they perceive as punishment has passed, the issue ought to be forgotten. This is not how women feel. In general, apologising is not good enough. A man must continue to demonstrate how sorry he is. The period of penance will vary in length from woman to woman.

However, if the woman continues to punish, in my experience she will, regrettably, enter what I call 'The Punishment Zone'. Unable to stop punishing her partner for the way she has been made to feel, a wronged woman may push him out of their relationship and into the arms of another woman.

It is a question of individual choice whether you forgive your partner and become reconciled. If you make the decision to forgive, there is little point in bringing up the adultery every time you have a row, for example, or being suspicious of their every move. This is bound to destroy your relationship.

**CASE STUDY** • • • • • • • • • • • • • •

Jerry had been married to Stella for fifteen years. When Stella noticed that Jerry was acting strangely, she decided to follow him, and saw him having coffee with Judy. Her suspicions aroused, she confronted her husband later that day. Jerry immediately confessed. He had been to bed with Judy, but only once. He was devastated about being discovered. Stella and their family meant everything to him. He apologised to Stella and promised that he would never stray again.

Jerry worked really hard to prove to Stella how very sorry he was. He was more attentive to her than ever and rang her regularly from work to reassure her. He took her away on short breaks and constantly told her how attractive and wonderful she was.

However, this was not enough. Stella had been shattered by Jerry's deception. She no longer trusted him. She rang him incessantly at work, wanting to know exactly where he was. If his secretary couldn't find him, Stella would drive to his office. If he was late home from work, she would accuse him of having started another affair. She became rude and offhand towards him, especially in front of his friends. The intensity of Stella's mistrust poisoned their relationship.

Eventually, Jerry lost his temper. He told Stella she was

just paying lip service to forgiving him and that she was really punishing him over and over again. Then he left her.

What Stella most feared was that Jerry would have another affair and leave her on her own. Because she was unable to conquer her fears, she unwittingly created the very situation that she did not want.

When Stella came to see me, she was completely distraught. She could not understand what Jerry had said. How could she be to blame when it was Jerry who had the affair and caused all the trouble, not her?

I suggested that Stella undergo therapy to help her cope with the situation. It was there that she understood what had really been happening. She contacted Jerry and asked if he would join her in therapy. She told him that she could see for the first time what he had been trying to tell her.

Jerry and Stella underwent therapy for a year. She learned to forgive Jerry and to trust him again. They are still married, but so nearly were not.

* * * * * * * * * * * * * * * * * * * * * *

If you find out that your partner has been unfaithful, you have the following choices:

1. You can choose to forgive your partner and rebuild your relationship.

2. You can choose to forgive them, but consult a therapist, marriage-guidance counsellor or psychologist to help you deal with the issues involved.

3. You can separate to give yourselves time to sort out how you feel.

4. You can divorce.

5. You can stay and continue to punish your partner, which may lead to Option 3 or 4.

The decision will obviously be taken out of your hands if your partner chooses to divorce or separate from you, regardless of your wishes.

Adultery is a serious matter which affects everyone in a family. If you are about to commit adultery, or confess to an affair, do stop and consider the impact your decision will have on those around you for the rest of your life. What dragons may you unleash, and what revenge?

# CHAPTER 12

# Revenge of the Dragon

*Heaven has no rage like love to hatred turned, no hell a fury like a woman scorned.*

– William Congreve

I often hear couples talk about how they love or hate the partner they want to stay with or divorce. The angry ones often express their desire for revenge for hurt feelings, particularly in situations where they have been betrayed or left by their partners. Revenge is a natural impulse, but one which, if unrealistic and unsatisfied, can do more to destroy the perpetrator than the original injury.

*Don't get mad, get even.*

– Ivana Trump

There are those who would say, 'Why should I not exact revenge? If my husband, wife or partner has deceived me and left, why should I not mete out a punishment to fit the crime, then I can feel better and move on?' The logic may be appealing, but the reality can be so different.

*Women and elephants never forget any injury.*

– Saki

In my experience, those who have exacted revenge in a dramatic manner have come to regret it later. This is because thereafter they are labelled as crazy, loopy or insane and the courts can impose sanctions upon them which have an impact for a long time, depriving them of the satisfaction that they hoped the revenge would bring them.

Revenge can take many forms, and may be described as follows:

1. Flamboyant revenge
2. Embarrassing revenge
3. Financial revenge
4. Social revenge

> *A woman's desire for revenge outweighs all of her other emotions.*
>
> – Cyril Connelly

# 1. Flamboyant Revenge

We have all heard stories about what those unrequited in love can do to each other. From glue on the toilet seat to laxatives in the coffee, they make amusing anecdotes for those dispensing the perceived punishment and a lifetime of embarrassment to those receiving it. There are, however, those who take matters much further and become imprisoned in a vortex of craving for revenge.

Following are some examples of flamboyant revenge, which, in the majority of cases, resulted in the courts awarding injunctions and costs against the perpetrators and making findings in financial hearings that matrimonial assets had been devalued or otherwise affected. Vengeance actually decreased the perpetrators' settlements or increased the amounts received by the recipients. Revenge was not at all sweet!

When a well-known personality discovered her husband was having an affair, she famously cut off the sleeves of each of his suits and gave away his prized vintage wine to all the neighbours. She felt great satisfaction at the time, knowing that her husband would feel utterly devastated about her handiwork. At the time, it gave her a sense of power in her otherwise powerless situation. However, just a short way into the legal process, she learned that her actions would be considered in the proceedings, which resulted in a financial settlement where she was so badly penalised that she felt as if she had been betrayed all over again. When asked about this, she is the first to admit that the desire for revenge certainly backfired in her case, although, in her old age, she says that she will spare herself the momentary grin as she remembers her husband's initial reaction.

Similarly, when Nadine found out that she had been betrayed by her husband – a member of the hunting, shooting and fishing brigade – she took her revenge. Knowing that her husband had a child-like adoration for his Baretta shotgun, which he painstakingly oiled and polished most weekends, she felt that there was only one way to let him know how she felt. She built a fire in the grate, put the gun in the centre and melted the barrel. Then, armed with the appropriate gloves and tools, she twisted and folded it beyond repair. She then cooled it, took it outside and drove over it with her Range Rover. She left the remains on his pillow, saying, 'Hope you sleep as well as you have allowed me to sleep.' The gun was worth approximately £10,000. The court granted her husband an injunction to stop her destroying anything else that belonged to him. She also was penalised for her actions.

Similarly, the wife who drove her husband's new Mercedes to a cliff, got out, took off the handbrake and allowed it to topple over the edge, found the full force of the law weighted against her when finances came to be dealt with. The car was worth approximately £60,000 and her capital claims were severely affected.

The wife who poured paint-stripper all over her estranged husband's car when she discovered his infidelity was found guilty of criminal damage, which, again, left her financially far worse off.

So, also, was the wife who arranged for a lorry load of manure to be delivered to her husband's mistress's home while the two of them were making love inside.

There have been many cases of clothes being attacked in one way or another. In many cases, sleeves of shirts and suits have been cut. Shirts have been knotted so that they cannot be unfolded, the flies of trousers or pyjamas have been tightly stitched or deliberately altered and put back in the cupboard only to be discovered at the last moment. In every case like this, the cost of the damage is deducted from any settlement or taken into account in any proceedings.

**CASE STUDY** •••••••••••••••

> Andy was due to have a celebratory golf match on Monday. On the Sunday before, Lucy discovered his long-term affair. He was out that day with his children from a previous marriage.
>
> Using his tool kit, she sawed through the top of each of his golf clubs, then arranged them back in his golf bag, covering them with the covers. As Andy went to take his first swing, he was immobilised with shock and the laughing stock of the entire golf club.
>
> Lucy managed to get temporary revenge – *until* Andy decided to get his. In a state of pique, Andy stuck all of her valuable stamp collection into her stamp book, rendering them worthless. Both of them faced injunction proceedings and a severe warning from the judge.

••••••••••••••••••••••

*An eye for an eye only leads to more blindness.*

– Margaret Atwood

## 2. Embarrassing Revenge

So many acts of embarrassing revenge involved in divorce cases have been perpetrated that they could fill a whole book by themselves. However, the following are from cases in which I have acted for the husband, wife or partner.

**CASE STUDIES** • • • • • • • • • • • • •

Estelle was very upset when she discovered that Barry had been cheating on her. She was given an anonymous tip-off and then decided to tape his calls. She discovered that he was arranging a liaison with his new girlfriend the following Wednesday at a London hotel to celebrate his birthday. The tape left Estelle in no doubt that they were to spend a very torrid lunchtime and afternoon together. Estelle was scorched by what she had heard and telephoned all of their friends, telling them that she was arranging a surprise birthday for Barry at the hotel that same day. She hoodwinked Reception into giving her a key for the room. She knew that Barry and his girlfriend had arranged to meet at 12.00. At one o'clock, Estelle opened the door, with all the friends shouting, 'Surprise!' For Barry and his girlfriend, it certainly was, and the end of a seven-year relationship for Estelle.

• • • • • • • • • • • •

Susan had been very let down by George's affair. The day he was due to move out and take his belongings from their home, he insisted that he also take the centre light that had been in their bedroom for ten years. As George took some of the boxes to his car, Susan popped a prawn into the light fitting. For months, George had every council authority official he could find investigating the smell coming from his new flat. He was unable to locate it until Susan gave the game away. She sent him a note saying, 'You left an odour in my life; I hope you like the one I left in yours.' George then went through everything he had taken from their home and discovered the decomposed prawn. George told me, after we had sorted their finances, that on the day of the settlement he had arranged for a plate of prawns to be delivered to her with a note, saying, 'I heard that revenge is a dish served best cold. I hadn't heard about prawns!' Both George and Susan can now laugh about the incident.

* * * * * * * * * * * *

Amy was so furious with Richard for leaving her that she arrived at his office in the city wearing a full-length mink coat, high heels and nothing else. She stormed into the boardroom where Richard was having a multinational meeting, flung open her coat and said, 'This is what Richard has given up!' She then turned on her heel and marched out. Interestingly, the visiting Chinese contingent didn't quite understand what was going on and believed it to be part of Richard's presentation. Richard was devastated and applied to the court for an injunction, which was granted to him to prevent Amy from ever visiting his offices or contacting him there again. Amy felt that she had had her revenge. It might have been different if the Chinese visitors had started to laugh during her performance as they did immediately afterwards, congratulating Richard on the most stimulating presentation that they had ever seen!

* * * * * * * * * * * *

Recently, there was a story in the newspapers which told of a vengeful wife who presented herself on stage during her husband's London theatre production, and told the audience of his affair. The audience thought it was part of the performance until the police arrived to remove her, and she was barred from going to the theatre again.

* * * * * * * * * * * *

Elaine telephoned Philip's office pretending she was from his surgery and giving him the results of his AIDS test. Philip was so embarrassed that for three weeks he could not even face going to work. In fact, although Philip accused Elaine of having made the call, he had no evidence to prove this and failed in his attempt to obtain an injunction against her.

* * * * * * * * * * * *

Similarly, when Peter split up from Janice, she arranged to anonymously send him a big box of Viagra pills via his receptionist at his law firm with a message to him taped to it that said: 'I do hope that this helps your problem. It must be really difficult for you, living with this – let me know – M.' Peter was teased for months afterwards at work, but, although he had his suspicions, he was never able to prove who sent it.

● ● ● ● ● ● ● ● ● ● ● ● ● ● ● ● ● ● ● ● ● ●

Some women choose to exact revenge by selling their stories to the press or writing books about their husband's indiscretions, particularly when they are high-profile men. From my experience of these situations, while the perpetrator experiences an immediate buzz and a sense of achievement, in most cases it has caused them long-lasting damage. The general public normally does not have respect for those who kiss and tell.

## 3. Financial Revenge

**CASE STUDY** ● ● ● ● ● ● ● ● ● ● ● ● ●

Simon was the head of a finance company and due to take out the company's most important client later that week. His girlfriend knew about this, but, unfortunately for Simon, she had also overheard a conversation in which Simon told someone he was intending to end his relationship with her. She exacted her revenge by cancelling all of their joint credit cards. When Simon went to pay the bill for his client, none of his cards could be authorised. In embarrassment, he had to arrange for his office to courier some cash to pay his bill – not exactly the kind of situation in which a financial advisor would wish to be found. Simon discovered the reason for his embarrassment when his girlfriend told him, as she packed her bags, that she hoped that it made him feel awful, because that was how she was feeling, and that his client would realise what a deceitful and misleading person he really was. Simon could do nothing, as she was perfectly in order to cancel the cards.

\* \* \* \* \* \* \* \* \* \* \* \* \* \* \* \* \* \* \* \* \* \*

Many women exact revenge via 'retail therapy'. They run up a large credit card bill or overdraft, believing that the way to get to a man is through his wallet. They believe merely threatening to part a man from his money will serve punishment or bring him back into line.

## CASE STUDIES \* \* \* \* \* \* \* \* \* \* \* \*

Genevieve exacted her revenge by spending up to the limit on every credit card she had when her relationship with her husband ended. She did not work, but he did, and earned meaningful sums. In the proceedings, her husband had to discharge all of her debts.

\* \* \* \* \* \* \* \* \* \* \* \*

When Isabel, who worked for similar wages to her husband, tried to exact the same revenge, however, it backfired. The judge found her spending to be excessive and unreasonable and ordered that she should be responsible for paying off all her family's credit card bills.

\* \* \* \* \* \* \* \* \* \* \* \*

Esther was a bitter woman. She had already been through three divorces. When she discovered Mitchell was having an affair, she donated £10,000 of their joint account to his boss's favourite charity. Esther believed that Mitchell would be too embarrassed to ask for it back, lest his boss found out. To her surprise, however, Mitchell did confide in his boss about her Machiavellian intentions and was able to retrieve his money. Esther was then put on the receiving end of an injunction which froze all of her money, and also severely reprimanded by the judge.

\* \* \* \* \* \* \* \* \* \* \* \* \* \* \* \* \* \* \* \*

# 4. Social Revenge

The best way in which women can obtain revenge of a kind which is not damaging to them – *and* brings the greatest reward – is through social matters. A woman may retain the friends she and her partner had during their relationship, and make sure that they will no longer wish to see the partner.

Alternatively, she may deprive her partner of the ability to discover anything about her social movements – what I call the 'silent social revenge'– or undergo the 'break-over social revenge'. This latter revenge is when her appearance or lifestyle has changed so much, that merely by seeing her or her success, her ex-partner is bound to regret his decision either to have started an affair or ending his relationship with her.

I have described the break-over in Chapter 7. This involves a complete change in appearance, from overweight to slim, from bad hair day to permanently perfect, from bad clothes year to enviably gorgeous lifetime.

There is, quite honestly, no better revenge than a woman's ex-partner to see her looking happy and gorgeous, and having a dismissive air about her, as if she has no need to give him a second thought. It is the ultimate and most stabbing punishment of all. So remember, *'Don't get mad; get gorgeous.'*

# 5. Frustrated Revenge

Over the last ten years, I have noticed that certain women suffer from mental stress when their relationships break down, and others from physical stress. This led me to wonder whether the causes for them were different. When I discovered the differences, I was both surprised and alarmed. Studies from the 1930s to date show that women who have unrealistic expectations – regarding their relationships, financial desires or revenge – will most certainly suffer from physical disorders. These may take the form of ulcers, gastrointestinal problems or irritable bowel disorders. While women may become temporarily distressed, and perhaps need tranquillisers and other stress relievers for a short time, these more frustrated women tend to have unrealistic expectations and no small desire for revenge.

A frustrated goal or the inability to exact revenge is more likely to cause physical illness than the break-up itself. Someone's frustration, thwarted plans for the future or unfulfilled quest for revenge are key factors. In 1984, Craig and Brown found in a study that divorced women more prone to anger and assertiveness, who do not simply accept a situation, were those most likely to become physically ill. I have found that men generally prefer to accept advice they are given in divorce proceedings rather than to actively fight their ex-partners, while women are four times more likely not to accept advice and to seek financial revenge.

I have found that battered women are particularly susceptible to health problems in circumstances where they are unable to obtain financial revenge through the courts that is commensurate with the misery they feel they have suffered. Those who have an unfulfilled desire for revenge are likely to experience deep frustration, which in turn leads to physical illness.

In my experience, it is infinitely better to let go of the idea and move on. Revenge is a dish which, unless easily and reasonably served, should be excluded from the menu altogether.

*No one delights more in vengeance than a woman.*
– Juvenal (60–130AD)

# CHAPTER 13

# Women and Violence

*In violence we forget who we are.*

– Mary McCarthy (1961)

Before you flick past this chapter, telling yourself: 'This has no relevance to me' – *Stop!* Right now, one of your friends or family may be suffering in an abusive relationship. If you understand why violence occurs, and the power play involved in it, you could be able to help.

There is a lot of ignorance about what makes men and women violent, and why people remain in abusive relationships. Public awareness of the issue is vital. People who have never experienced an abusive situation are often too quick to judge and condemn people involved in one because they have no notion whatsoever of the range of emotions or difficulties experienced by both parties. This is because those who have not been in this situation are judging life by their own limited experiences and standards which they believe to be correct. They are blind to the fact that others may be experiencing what they will never encounter.

Situations like the ones I mention below are very familiar to me in my work as a matrimonial lawyer. I share them in the hope that:

1. If you are the victim of an abusive partner, you will see that you do have choices.
2. If you are a friend or relative of somebody in this situation, you will be better equipped to help them.

Everybody has choices. If you choose to stay in, or condone, an abusive relationship without trying to change it, then you are to blame for your continuing misery.

It is now a fact that violence or battering is distributed throughout the social classes, at all levels. It has been shown that men in their thirties and forties are more likely to batter their partners than any other age group. Domestic or family violence has increased threefold in the last ten years, and there has been a substantive increase in battering among the middle classes. There has also been a marked increase in the numbers of men who admit they have been habitually abused by women.

These facts have been thrust into the public gaze by the media over the last few years. There are those who suggest that the figures for domestic violence have always been the same and that it is simply the media that has brought them to our attention, but the numbers have undoubtedly risen. If one looks at the underlying causes of domestic violence, it is clear that these have increased in line with statistics.

Analysing the divorce petitions made in Britain over the last five years does not shed any light on these statistics, because they do not accurately reflect what goes on behind closed doors. Divorce petitions are, in reality, an artificial method of bringing an already broken marriage to an end. In Britain, unlike most other European countries and the USA, grounds for divorce must be established. For a divorce to be granted, it must be proven that a marriage has irretrievably broken down and that at least one of the following applies:

- One party has committed adultery and the other finds it intolerable to live with them.
- One party has behaved in such a way that the other cannot be reasonably expected to live with them.

- One party has deserted the other for a continuous period of two years.
- Both parties have separated for at least two years and both consent to a divorce.
- The parties have been separated for five years.

Violence falls into the second category. However, because it is the British government's intention to abolish grounds for divorce, British judges are already directing lawyers not to mention domestic violence or be seen to be acrimonious when dealing with divorce petitions. Lawyers are actively encouraged to omit any grounds which might invite controversy. Accordingly, there has been a drop in the number of women and men referring to violence in divorce petitions and, indeed, anywhere in the proceedings. Some women who have been victims of domestic violence resent that their experiences have not been made public; the impact of this elsewhere in society has been building for many years.

Only those with first-hand experience of domestic violence can appreciate the numbers involved and the impact that it has on a family, and the wide range of emotions people have in such situations.

> *The Canadians have declared that domestic violence is not a feminist issue but a matter of human rights.*
> – Caroline Moorhead (1991)

In a book by Jean Renvoize called *Web of Violence*, the author refers to a report by a consultant forensic psychiatrist, Dr. Faulk, which places men who have violent relationships with their wives in five distinct categories:

### Category 1
*Dependent passive men whose attempts to pacify their*

*querulous, dominating wives break down, sometimes under
direct provocation, resulting in a violent attack.*

Dr. Faulk's research confirms previous findings that such
men can be passive, indecisive and sexually inadequate,
and their female partners aggressive and even masculine
in their behaviour. These studies describe how women
may take over the running of the household to prevent
their husbands overspending and to ensure that vital
decisions are taken. The wife becomes responsible for all
that happens in the household. When things go wrong,
the husband generally blames the wife, and he considers
himself justified in physically abusing her.

## Category 2

*The dependent but suspicious type of man who is very
jealous of his wife, usually unjustly.*

A man's jealousy can build up and erupt in ever-increas-
ing violence, with the battering husband feeling a need to
have complete power over his wife. Often his jealousy is
of a sexual nature, and reflects his doubt about his own
potency. Faulk refers to a report by Dr. Gayford, who
found that such men constantly accuse their wives of infidelity and in many cases the jealousy is delusory. Since
half of the men he interviewed had had affairs during
their marriage, Gayford suggested that these husbands
might be projecting their own behaviour onto their
innocent wives. Delusional jealousy is particularly dangerous, since it is fruitless to argue with the accuser.

## Category 3

*Violent and bullying.*

## Category 4

*Dominating men with a strong need to prove themselves.*

Category 5

> *Husbands with a stable and affectionate relationship with their wives who have, during a period of severe mental disturbance, assaulted them.*

Within these categories, domestic violence differs in severity and type. These types can be categorised as:

- Destructive Violence
- 'One-off' Violence
- Alcohol-related Violence

# Destructive Violence

This is the most dangerous type of violence, where the goal is to control or punish. It usually involves other forms of abusive behaviour as well. Abusers will, for example, use verbal attacks to destroy their partner's self-confidence, and provoke fear by making threats. They also often subject their partners to severe, malicious, emotional and psychological bullying and themselves exhibit irrational jealousy. Victims may be unable to leave a bad situation due to lack of money, debt, worries or concern about their children. But this is not always the case. Destructive violence is prevalent in middle– or upper-class families and among certain ethnic groups.

'Often,' says Julian Nettlefield in his book, *Saving the Situation*, 'the instrumental abuser will be popular with others and seem charming in public life, only showing the full panoply of abusive behaviours behind closed doors.' He may have a prestigious career and be respected in his community. This type of abuser is unlikely to regard aggression and violence as wrong or to feel guilty about using it. The abuser maintains financial control in the family and resents his partner enjoying life in any way. Such people also tend to be excessively jealous of their partners' relationship with their children.

## CASE STUDY ● ● ● ● ● ● ● ● ● ● ● ● ● ● ●

Julian was a successful lawyer from a well-known and respected family. He was a few years older than Vivian when they met. At the time, she was studying to become an accountant. From the beginning of their marriage, Julian took out on his wife his frustrations about the legal cases he dealt with. If a case went well, he was happy, but if it went badly, he would hit her.

The situation worsened after the birth of their first child. Julian was very jealous and would do everything he could to distract Vivian from their child; he would demand his evening meal, or insist that she fetch things for him whenever she tried to feed the baby or change its nappies. His behaviour degenerated into that of a vicious, spoilt child. The harder Vivian tried, the nastier Julian became. The beatings grew in severity. He would deliberately find fault at home, pointing out things for her to do. When he came home from work, if she had prepared beef for dinner, for example, he would insist he had told her in the morning that he wanted fish. He would hide things, then demand that she find them for him, insisting that she had lost them. He would start arguments with her while she was in the bath and then strike her across the back repeatedly if she disagreed with him. He would tell her over and over again that she was unattractive and stupid. If they went on holiday together, he would sit next to her on the beach and tell her how repulsive she looked compared to all the other women.

Vivian knew that the things he was saying were untrue, but, because he was so convincing, her confidence in herself slowly evaporated and she began to believe him. Julian kept Vivian isolated from her family and friends, telling her how they despised, hated and were jealous of her. She became increasingly nervous and ill. She would constantly diet, even though she was only a size ten.

Then Vivian qualified as an accountant and started to

become successful. She was able to do so by, effectively, becoming two people. At work, she adopted the persona of a confident, successful accountant, projecting an aura of strength, which was the complete antithesis of the way she behaved at home. As soon as she returned home, however, she reverted to the role of the insecure, fearful victim. The more successful she became, the more abusive Julian became. For instance, after their child's birthday parties, he routinely destroyed the child's gifts after their guests had left, then would tell Vivian that it was her fault: *she* had made him lose his temper.

One day, Vivian had a car accident and suffered severe whiplash. That night, while she was in agony, she asked Julian to take her to the hospital.

Julian replied he was far too busy working on a case to take her to hospital. He told her that it was 'wicked and unreasonable' of her to expect him to do so, then struck her.

Vivian managed to get her father to take her to the hospital. While they were waiting for a doctor, she noticed a couple sitting next to her.

The man was holding the woman's hand; she had an injury similar to Vivian's. He was trying to comfort her, telling her that she would be all right and that he would look after her.

In that instant, Vivian saw Julian as he really was, and realised that she was totally alone. All the terrible things that he had said to her seemed to dance before her eyes. Suddenly she knew she had to remove herself from what was a dreadful situation.

Vivian divorced Julian and six months later found a new partner. Since the divorce, Vivian has gone from strength to strength. She has learned that in order to stop being a victim, she had to stop seeing herself as one. After realising this, she never became one again. Now she is an extremely successful accountant and a very happily married wife and mother, and has never looked back.

Vivian says she hopes that her story will encourage people who are in the same situation. 'There is another life if you want to take it,' she says.

Of the five categories of violence described by Dr. Faulk, Category 1 has been found to be the most common. It is regrettable that Dragon Women sometimes inadvertently provoke a cycle of domestic violence that can lead to the demise of a relationship. I am not suggesting that violence in any form is acceptable, because I believe it is not, but it may be possible to avoid it. The irrational perception that she has to take charge of everything in the home often leads to further feelings of inadequacy in a woman's partner. She may 'over-mother' him to such an extent that he becomes incapable of doing anything for himself. This sets up a pattern of doing, inadequacy, more doing, resentment, then violence. Unfortunately, both partners often refuse to accept any responsibility for provoking the other's behaviour. They have become co-dependent, trapped in a cycle of negative behaviour. If you are in this category, I would suggest that you seek help from a psychotherapist to work out strategies, with or without your partner, that will enable you to break free of this unhappy cycle.

> *If human beings are to survive in a nuclear age,*
> *committing acts of violence may eventually have to*
> *become as embarrassing as urinating or defecating in*
> *public are today.*
>
> – Miriam Miedzian

By continuously undermining a passive, ineffectual man, a domineering woman can create an abusive situation – one that is abhorrent and overwhelming for both of them. The choices open to a woman in such a plight are clear:

1. She can stop behaving like a Dragon Woman, using the self-help methods suggested in this book.
2. She can try to talk to her partner about their problems

and how they can both change – how she can become less aggressive and he less ineffectual.

3. She can remove herself from the relationship altogether.

For a woman with a partner in Category 2 (dependent, suspicious and jealous), the options are as follows:

1. Discuss your partner's unreasonable jealousy with him, and find a method of reassuring him that you are not flirting with other men and have no desire to be with anyone else.

2. Undertake some form of therapy together with your partner that will address your problems and how to avoid them.

3. You can leave him.

4. You can continue to take the abuse until you are worn out and become ill.

The partner of a man in Category 3 (violent and bullying) may be subjected to one of several kinds of abuse. For example, in his book, *Saving the Situation*, Julian Nettlefield describes 'the physically violent, where genetic or family dispositions may have drawn the victim to subconsciously marry an abuser'. This means that if you have come from a home where domestic violence was routine, you are more likely to become the victim of violence or an aggressive abuser.

**CASE STUDY** ● ● ● ● ● ● ● ● ● ● ● ● ● ● ●

John, the son of a headmaster, was brought up in a very strict environment. He was often caned by his father for bad behaviour. A short time after he started a relationship with Gail, John became abusive towards her. He regularly hit her if things were not going his way, particularly when he had been drinking. Normally he was a fairly passive man, but after a few drinks he would come home and hit Gail. He began to do this with increasing force, and sometimes broke things around the home. Gail found this more and more difficult and embarrassing to cover up. John wouldn't hit Gail anywhere that would show, restricting his blows to the parts of her body that were usually covered by clothing.

Gail loved John, but when she could no longer put up with his violent behaviour, she came to visit me with a view to instigating divorce proceedings. An injunction had to be obtained on one occasion because John had assaulted her so badly; he had pulled her downstairs by her hair and kicked her back so hard that her spine was injured.

After the injunction had been obtained, Gail tearfully told me that she wanted the marriage to work. John was referred to a specialist who helped him stop drinking after he and Gail were referred to a psychotherapist, who came up with a feasible game plan to help them deal with the situation. Both of them were taught skills designed to avoid confrontational situations in the future and learned to recognise warning signs in order to sidestep conflict. John came to understand that, instead of using his hands or his belt, as his father had on him, he should discuss his feelings with Gail. They realised that walking away from the situation until both of them had calmed down was the way forward. Gail confessed that at times she provoked John by her behaviour. She said she 'knew which buttons to press to make him go mad' and yet she had frequently done so anyway. They are still happily married.

* * * * * * * * * * * * * * * * * * * * * *

# One-off Violence

Nettlefield identifies a form of violence where an argument between partners results in one of them committing an aggressive act. During the argument, they both may push and shove each other, or throw things. The roles of aggressor and victim are not fixed in this scenario. However, if this kind of violence is allowed to recur, and coupled with a tendency towards excessive drinking or some additional factor that creates frustration, it may become increasingly unpleasant. Quite often, couples in this category have experienced a sudden family bereavement, illness, change of home, loss or impending loss of a job, stress or pregnancy.

I call this 'the one-off outburst'; when the underlying stress disappears, so will the problem. Often someone in this situation will instigate divorce proceedings but fail to continue with them once the problem is gone. People who fall into this category have the following choices:

1. They can leave their partner. (However, they may forever regret having failed to give the relationship a second chance.)

2. They can both seek help – from a marriage-guidance counsellor or couples therapist – to ensure that the violence never recurs.

3. They can continue to behave as before and, if there is another violent incident, consider the above options.

## Alcohol-related Violence

Also found in the violent and bullying category are those predisposed towards excessive drinking. There is a proven link between alcohol abuse and domestic violence. We do not know whether this is because the kind of person who is liable to resort to violence, due to poor self-control, low self-esteem, natural irritability, etc., will also tend to seek support or solace in alcohol. Alternatively, is it that men who would not otherwise be violent take to drink because of frustrations at work or at home and, as a result, lose their normal inhibitions against aggression?

Dr. Gayford found that 44 per cent of husbands who regularly get drunk beat their wives. Men who are prescribed tranquillisers on a regular basis can be predisposed towards violent outbursts, and a quarter of men with drinking problems who batter their wives also have gambling problems.

A woman whose partner fits into this category has the following choices:

1. If her partner is willing to recognise that he has a problem, both must seek professional help – from Alcoholics Anonymous, Gamblers Anonymous, for example, or a qualified therapist.

2. If her partner will not seek help, she must decide whether she is prepared to remain in this cycle of abuse; leaving may be the only solution.

According to Julian Nettlefield, if a sudden outburst of anger is frightening, unprovoked, causes stress and is not followed by any evidence of remorse, there is a possibility that the person has a personality disorder. Some research suggests that, because that part of the brain is immature, someone who has such a disorder will behave rather like a spoilt child, denying that they are at fault and blaming other people, society, etc. If you are the partner of such a person, you have the following options:

1. You can seek help together with your partner.

2. Your partner can undergo tests to show whether there is some underlying medical cause for his violent outbursts.

3. You can leave him.

4. You can continue to deal with your partner's violence, which may in time adversely affect your own health.

Nowadays the number of women abusers in the violent and

bullying category is growing. They are often diagnosed as 'borderline' or 'histrionic' personalities. Borderline personalities are quick to anger, very demanding, attention-seeking, impulsive and dramatic. They also tend to be manipulative and shallow.

Someone whose partner persistently displays such behaviour has the following options:

1. Talk to him and decide whether the problems between you can be overcome through some form of joint therapy.

2. If your partner is unwilling to undergo any form of therapy or counselling, you must decide whether or not to remain in the relationship.

3. If there could be an underlying hormonal reason for your partner's behaviour, you should seek proper medical assistance.

4. You can refer the issue to your local domestic violence unit (attached to most police stations) and be registered as being at risk.

5. You can seek legal advice about whether an injunction can be taken out against your partner to prevent him behaving in the same way again or, in very violent situations, to have him removed from your home.

## Outside Intervention

Domestic violence units, which are attached to most police stations, are a recent phenomenon. They have proved to be very effective in some areas.

Domestic violence was previously thought to be a domestic matter and the police very rarely intervened. In recent years, domestic violence has been recognised as an identifiable criminal offence and the police now have the power to arrest and imprison offenders. It is also possible for a court to order a power of arrest to be attached to orders for injunctions which again enables the police to act at once, without any further application to the court.

Whatever the powers of the courts and police, most people in these situations are afraid to involve the authorities. Many believe this will have little positive effect on the situation, and could even make it worse.

**CASE STUDY** ● ● ● ● ● ● ● ● ● ● ● ● ● ● ●

Sam had been married to Jean for a year before he realised that she was extremely volatile. As the years progressed, Jean's volatility turned into violence. She would become argumentative, particularly when she was pre-menstrual, and strike him about the head, calling him 'useless', 'hopeless' and 'a waste of space'. Once she threw paint-stripper over Sam's new car because she said he had been spending too much time on it. On another occasion, she drove over his golf-clubs, then used one of the clubs to hit him on the leg. When Sam told one of his friends that Jean was hitting him, his friend laughed. Sam became more enclosed in his own unhappy world, too embarrassed to tell anyone that he was going through hell.

When Sam came to see me, he sat at my desk and cried as he told me his story. He kept apologising for telling me what he had been going through. He had been victimised and abused for so long that he even felt he had to act the victim to his own lawyer. Sam was worried that no one would believe Jean had hit him. She was slightly built and nearly a foot shorter than him. When the case came before the magistrates' court, Jean's lawyer laughed as he asked Sam to stand up. He said: 'Are you seriously suggesting that this woman could perpetrate such violence upon you, a strapping man of six foot two?' All the police officers sitting in court were grinning too. This lasted until Sam's barrister gently provoked Jean into a show of temper. After five minutes of listening to Jean furiously screaming and swearing from the witness box, realisation dawned. The smiles faded. The court found that Jean had been violent towards Sam and made restraining orders against her. Sam found the strength to leave home. He is now in a new relationship, and very happy.

●●●●●●●●●●●●●●●●●●●●●●●

# The Victim-Aggressor Syndrome

Research has clearly shown that many women who become the victims of domestic violence have come from families where the father was dominant. They are often bubbly, warm and affectionate people who are desperate to please, anxious to win or keep their partner. They are normally also desperately insecure. When they find themselves in an abusive situation, they will try hard to find a solution and even harder to gain the love of the person who is abusing them. This is a factor that most people cannot understand.

Many victims find themselves in a continuous triangular situation of abuse, victimisation and further abuse. The abuser will abuse the victim. The abuser will convince the victim that he/she is responsible for the abuse so that the abuser cannot stop themselves from harming him/her. The victim will then believe that he/she is the only person who can save the abuser, redoubling his/her efforts to do so. This will lead to a continuous triangle of abuse, victimisation and abuse.

The pattern of behaviour between the actress Pamela Anderson her husband Tommy Lee was typical of the Victim/ Aggressor syndrome. Although she was being abused, Ms. Anderson sincerely believed that she was the key to her husband's redemption. She did in fact leave him for a while, but then went back to him to try to help him.

So often in situations of domestic abuse, it is not the violence that is most destructive, but the verbal abuse. As we have seen, a characteristic of an abuser (usually a man) is to isolate the victim from all her relatives and friends, thus obtaining total power over her. The victim will then believe that everything she is told is correct. It is sometimes difficult for people who have not encountered this situation to understand how highly intelligent women, from every social class, can be convinced that they are stupid, unworthy, ignorant, fat, unattractive, hopeless, helpless, inefficient, useless mothers, employees, wives, etc., when everyone else can see only clear evidence to the contrary. The victim, who is fed a daily diet of threats and criticism, believes what she is told because she is extremely insecure. She is convinced that she is stupid, incompetent and to blame for everything that is going wrong, because her abuser tells her so, and thus becomes unable to escape from the situation and make a new life for herself. It is the victim's perception of herself as helpless, stupid and incompetent that keeps so many battered women at home.

However, I can state with authority that each and every woman who manages to break free from an abusive situation will become more successful than she would have dared to hope. I call this 'The Phoenix Syndrome'; it is the ability of a woman to rise from the ashes of an abusive relationship to start again and to become successful. To those women (and men) who cannot believe it is possible to begin again, and who think they lack the power or resources to do so, I would say: 'Take a good look at your situation. Who is the real you? What is your partner really like?'

In order to help clients of mine who face this situation, I have devised a 'reality test'. In Oscar Wilde's play, *The Picture of Dorian Gray*, a young man sells his soul to the devil in exchange for remaining young for ever. He can behave as wickedly as he wishes and he will always be young, handsome, rich and successful. However, in the attic of his house is a portrait that reflects how he truly is and how he is developing. With every evil act he perpetrates, the painting becomes uglier. At the end of the book, when Dorian Gray faces his portrait, he turns into the hideous, twisted character in the picture.

If you are a victim, try to see what kind of person you are really married to or living with. Imagine your partner's picture in the attic – the real picture of him/her. Imagine – not the person who is in front of you, who is convincing you of what he is like, but – the person he really is. When you are able to see the person's true picture, you will be able to make the right decision about your relationship. Do you wish to remain in it, and seek help, or escape from the person in the painting?

## Family, Friends and Outsiders

It is often extremely difficult to be an outsider looking in on an abusive situation. To you, the answer is obvious: the person should remove themselves immediately from the abusive situation.

If, however, the victim loves the abuser and sees him as a necessary part of her family, as a father to her children, for example, the decision to simply remove herself from the situation is a difficult one, which she must consider carefully.

Telling an abused person that she must immediately remove herself from the situation will usually make her defensive about the abuser. She will automatically try to save her partner from criticism. She will also be reluctant to admit to herself or others that she has made a terrible mistake in her choice of partner.

Therefore, if you are the parent or friend of a victim of abuse, you must listen to what they have to say, rather than tell them what you think. Your expressed abhorrence of the situation may lead them to remain in that situation far longer.

Your insistence that they must leave may give rise to further feelings of inadequacy. Afraid that they will not be able to cope outside the abusive situation, they may cling to it all the more.

## Life After Abuse

It is my hope that, having investigated all the options available, if you are a victim you will understand that there is life after abuse. You will be successful, you will cope, and you and your children will be better off without your abusive partner. If your situation falls into the violent category, or the one-off violence category, your decisions must be much more carefully weighed.

If you choose to stay in an abusive situation, you must develop the skills to deal with it. As we have seen, some women who are the victims of abuse actually encourage their partner's aggressive and violent behaviour. If you have been in an abusive situation, you may perpetuate the same cycle of abuse in subsequent relationships unless you seek help. In therapy, you may come to realise that you have a predisposition towards becoming a victim in any relationship and are trying too hard to be loved. You will be taught how to look at your relationship in a more rational and calm way to prevent any recurrence of this cycle.

It is important, for example, to convert irrational thoughts into positive ones. If you are being told that you are stupid, ignorant and unattractive, when this is simply untrue, you must learn not to be affected by such statements. They are coming from someone who is insecure and unworthy. If you understand that the hurtful things such a person says have absolutely no validity, they will cease to have the power to affect you. You should then be able to rise out of your victim status and either leave, or help to mend, the relationship.

It is my experience that if a person in an abusive situation alters her perceptions and behaviour, it can change. It is crucial to understand that by adopting certain postures and approaches during a dangerous build-up of tension, a victim often promotes abuse. Where partners do not wish their relationship to end, despite the violence, they may be able to turn it around by changing their own automatic reactions to the other person's behaviour. From the cases I have seen, tendencies to cringe, cry, go into the foetal position or adopt other childlike behaviours can arouse violent reactions. Men have described how their total inability to deal with such behaviour leads them to lash out.

Many abusers have told me that if their partners plead, beg and behave like frightened children, they chastise or smack them as if dealing with a naughty child. So often a victim will prolong an argument, refusing to stop until her partner hits her. By learning to avoid shouting 'dog and boning' in these dangerous situations, victims can avoid being abused.

Therapists suggest taking a very calm approach. Do not cringe or shout; try quiet, clear reasoning. If, after a short time, the situation becomes heated, you must walk away; otherwise, you will create the very thing you fear. You must stop behaving like a victim and falling into victim mode, because this will trigger aggression in your partner.

When one of my clients was told by a therapist to stop being a victim, she was devastated. She felt that she was not the one to be blamed or whose behaviour should change. When she realised that she must alter her whole perception of the situation and her body language, things did improve, however. When she stopped acting the victim, her partner stopped acting the aggressor and her life changed completely. It is, therefore, possible to remain in such a situation, *but only if both partners work towards making changes*. However, if you do your part to stop triggering conflict and your partner continues to use violence against you, I would unhesitatingly advise you to leave.

Domestic abuse is one of the most agonising situations anyone can experience. The decisions that have to be taken are not always easy, but there *are* options. Those options should be carefully considered and then acted upon. The most important question you should ask yourself is, 'What do I want?'

*Blows are fitter for beasts than rational creatures.*
                                                    – Hannah Woolley (1675)

# CHAPTER 14

# What Do Women Want?

*The great question which I have not been able to answer, despite my thirty years of research into the feminine soul, is 'What does a woman want?'*

– Sigmund Freud

Throughout this book, I have emphasised what men want from their relationships with women, and how women misunderstand men. However, a complete picture of relationships could not be formed without setting out what women want from their relationships also (although some of these issues have already been dealt with earlier in this book).

Women can express their emotional needs very easily but often they feel that they are not heard. From the thousands of cases in which I have been involved, I have come to the conclusion that the following are what most women want from their relationships. When women believe that they are not receiving the following, they will wish to end a relationship.

## Women Want Love to be Expressed Daily

*What is irritating about love is that this is a crime that requires an accomplice.*

– Charles Baudelaire

A woman is not content to remember that last week her partner told her that he loved her. She wants to be told this repeatedly.

Women believe that men should overtly demonstrate their love with actions or words on a daily basis. While men believe that settling down with women or paying the mortgage is the greatest act of love they can possibly demonstrate, this is not generally sufficient for most women. Women crave reassurance. Because they give reassurance and love so openly and freely to men and have a natural instinct to want to please them, they cannot understand why they should face cold, non-affectionate responses from them.

Men must remember one basic rule: 'A cuddle a day keeps the lawyer away.' Women like physical closeness. This does not mean that they immediately want sex too. They quite often just need physical contact which reassures them that you love or care about them.

So often in divorce cases, I find that men and women complain that they have not had physical contact of any kind for years. They live in a cold clinical environment, simply being polite to their partners until all affection between them dies. Women need regular physical contact, which gives them the reassurance they need. One warm cuddle can do more than interminable cold discussions. If a woman suggests you cuddle, do not do this grudgingly, as if it is some big favour that you are doing for her, or else the cuddle will go no way at all to giving her the reassurance she needs.

During your courtship before you moved in together or were married, you probably showered her with affection by giving her little gifts or telephoning to her just to say hello, I love you or I miss you. Often once a relationship becomes more permanent, men give up doing these things. Because men feel more secure in the relationship as time goes by, they do not see any need to follow these 'courtship rituals'.

However, when you take away something that a woman has been used to, she misses it dreadfully. Men must demonstrate their love during the whole of a relationship to succeed on the 'approval scale'. This can take many forms such as:

- Remembering her birthday
- Remembering your anniversary
- Remembering your children's birthdays
- Remembering to book a restaurant
- Remembering to book a holiday
- If you remember her mother's birthday, you will score very high points on her approval scale
- Remembering to ask how she got on when she visited the doctor
- Going with her to visit the doctor
- Helping her with the children
- Helping her around the home
- Telling her that she looks wonderful
- Telling her that she is brilliant at work.

Forgetting these things indicates to her that you do not care and have not even given her a thought. Women will disasterise considerably if these things happen all the time.

> *A husband is what is left of a lover once the nerve has been extracted.*
>
> – Helen Roland

## Showing Interest in a Woman

The reason why so many women constantly ask annoying questions like 'Is anything the matter?' is because they see that their partner is very quiet and believe that they have been responsible for it. This is because women gauge men's behaviour by relating it to their own. Because this is how women would behave if they were annoyed with their partner, they superimpose their perspective upon it. However, the question is really shorthand for 'You have not been talking to me and I need some form of communication to stop feeling so nervous and unloved'. Women cannot bear empty time or space and instinctively want to fill them up. They also feel threatened when their partners look at other women. Both of you must try to understand the other's point of view in order to avoid unnecessary arguments due to this behaviour.

*Any time that is not spent on love is wasted.*
– Toquato Tasso

Women hate men going into thinking cave mode where they feel shut out. While John Gray tells us that we should give men time to emerge, most women are impatient and cannot cope well with the long silences – which are alien to them. So, before you go into a very long quiet spell in which you do not wish your partner to be a space invader, do the following: give her a hug and say, 'There are some things I am mulling over right now. Please give me a short time alone, then I would love to hear about your day.' This is the kind of language that women understand. It will comfort them, and they will be satisfied for a while. However, when you stop churning the events of your day, spare a thought for a woman's need to offload. Provided that she is prepared to follow my advice about communication and timetables so that you are not worn to a frazzle, do try to bend a bit to accommodate her. Learn the 'Umm technique' so that you can look and sound as if you are listening so she does not feel cut off and frustrated. Adding the occasional 'I think you are great' will probably last two to three days on the approval scale. You can certainly tell if a woman is happy; her fists will be unclenched, she will usually be smiling and occasionally she will hum. If she is standing stiffly, her hands clenched and her arms and legs crossed, there is something troubling her greatly. A woman is far more likely to respond if she feels that you are taking an interest in her. Such a woman feels nurtured and is more likely to grow with you in a relationship and will want to repay you five times over by affection and kindness. If a woman feels shut off and of little importance, she will become frustrated; this will grow into a pattern of resentment and a desire to do less for you.

**CASE STUDY** ✦ ✦ ✦ ✦ ✦ ✦ ✦ ✦ ✦ ✦ ✦ ✦ ✦ ✦

> Brenda had been trying to talk to Kenneth for months. Every time she tried to talk to him about problems at work or difficulties with the children, Kenneth would hold up his hand as if to say 'Silence'. Brenda tried to understand that Kenneth needed to unwind after work, but any time she approached him to talk, he seemed uninterested in listening to her. Brenda was frustrated and lonely. She felt that she was a lone soul battling against the elements instead of half of a couple facing the world together.
>
> Most evenings Kenneth would finish his dinner then play on his computer. He regularly e-mailed his friends and generally cut himself off from Brenda and their family. Eventually, Brenda had had enough. One day she e-mailed him at work saying, 'You tune into your e-mail, what a shame you never tuned into me.' Kenneth was totally amazed at Brenda's outburst but it was too late and the marriage was beyond repair.

✦ ✦ ✦ ✦ ✦ ✦ ✦ ✦ ✦ ✦ ✦ ✦ ✦ ✦ ✦ ✦ ✦ ✦ ✦ ✦ ✦

## Women Need to Be Able to Exaggerate Events to Their Partner Without Criticism

Women fantasise much more than men about their lives. They are taught to do this from a very early age, whereas men are taught to have a much more direct and realistic approach to life. A woman does not want to feel boring or unimportant. Therefore, to avoid this, she will often dramatise events:

a. In the hope that you will take more notice of her
b. To make life more exciting.

It is very important that men recognise that this is a trait of many women. While most of their worries can be countered by turning their negative thoughts to positive ones, men can go further to help. Avoid telling women that they are drama queens. Try to accept that this is a woman's shorthand way of saying, 'I need to be heard. I need you to sympathise. I need you to deal with the situation for me or tell me I got it right.' Men often regard these exaggerations as criticisms of them. They are not always meant to be, but are rather a measure of a woman's self-esteem at any given time.

> *Falling in love consists merely in uncorking the imagination and bottling the common sense.*
>
> – Helen Rowland

## Women Want to Be Listened to

> *Men are not against you, they are merely for themselves.*
>
> – Jean Fowler

Many women in divorce proceedings claim that their male partners do not listen to them and are constantly cutting them off, leaving them feeling frustrated. They say that they are not allowed to have views, that men always want to be right and that sometimes the only place where they feel heard is at work.

Earlier in this book, I approached this problem from men's perspective. However, it is certainly the case in many instances that some men behave in a belligerent and belittling manner, particularly in relation to a woman's successful career. Men too, must recognise that it is unfair to expect your partner to always build you up and to never expect to reciprocate. If, as a man, you feel resentful of your partner's career, you must look carefully at your reasons for it and try to address them. If you continue to put her down and destroy her confidence, then you will push her into the arms of another man.

Wives seem more likely to have affairs when partners' careers compete. It seems obvious to me that if you continuously find fault with someone who is made to feel good by everyone around her at work, she will want to off-load the part of her life that is giving her grief, so be warned!

This also applies to women at home who are constantly belittled and crave reassurance; they will actively look for someone else who makes them feel better.

## Women Want to Feel Attractive

Women need to be told constantly how sexy and attractive they are. We live in a world where appearances are so important, so make the effort to remember to praise her. Not noticing her hair style or new outfit is tantamount to saying, 'I don't notice you because you're not worth noticing.' She will feel very disappointed and let down. When women are made to feel sexy, they are more likely to behave in a sexy manner. As I have indicated in Chapter 6, for women sex starts in the head and spreads south. If a woman feels pampered, attractive, sexy and alluring, she will feel happy and is more likely to want sex.

If she is never told that she is attractive or is teased about her appearance constantly, she will close up like a flower deprived of sunlight.

*Women are never disarmed by compliments. Men always are. That is the difference between the sexes.*

– Oscar Wilde

**CASE STUDY** ●●●●●●●●●●●●●●

Laura was an attractive woman, but at home she felt flat, boring and plain. Her partner Simon never paid her a compliment about her looks and rarely seemed to notice her. She tried changing her hairstyle several times and buying different outfits – anything, just to get his attention. To Laura, Simon always seemed preoccupied. If she pointed out her new hairstyle, he would mumble, 'Yeah, great.'

One day, Laura was wearing a dress she had owned for five years, and worn on countless occasions, and Simon remarked 'New dress?' Laura was incensed. She felt so unnoticed and unloved that she felt that she was Shirley Valentine. She said that she often found herself fantasising conversations with her kitchen wall, asking the wall things like, 'Hello wall, what do you think of my new outfit?' The wall would often respond that she looked gorgeous, but Simon never did. One day, Laura replaced the wall by talking to her next-door neighbour, who was a bachelor. He told her that he thought her new hairstyle really suited her. Laura said that she felt more alive than she had in years. She started an affair with him and left Simon. Laura said that she had tried very hard to obtain any sort of reaction from Simon, but that there was only one person in their relationship, not two.

●●●●●●●●●●●●●●●●●●●●●

# Women Want to Feel Secure

Women love to feel secure. There is nothing that makes a woman feel so good as when she is loved and appreciated by her partner. Treating her in a way that makes her feel the opposite is bound to cause her distress. Coming home very late without explanation will make her feel insecure and suspect that you are seeing someone else. Lying to her when you are being constantly found out will certainly lead to great insecurity.

An insecure woman is twice as likely to overwhelm you with questions in an attempt to gain your reassurance than one who is already reassured. Do not, therefore, blame the woman if your actions have given rise to or exacerbated her insecurity. Telephoning your partner from the office occasionally just to say 'Hello, I miss you' can do wonders for a woman's security and happiness.

> *Security is mortals' chiefest enemy.*
>
> – Ellen Terry

## Women Want to Trust their Partners

Trust means a great deal to a woman. Women are built to put everything into their relationships – to the extent that they can become part of their whole reason for being. Therefore being able to trust their partners is paramount in importance to them. When that trust is broken, it is extremely difficult for a woman to regain it and if broken repeatedly can lead some women floundering for the rest of their lives from its ill effects. If you can understand why trust is so important to a woman, then you will understand its effects when it is broken.

## Women Want Commitment

Women crave commitment from their men in the same way that they crave and require trust. Without the essence of commitment, a woman does not feel able to put into the relationship what she would, ideally, like to give. If she believes that the relationship is transient, she is fearful of giving all of herself and facing rejection as a consequence. If you give so much into a relationship that the other person becomes the centre of your universe, it is far harder to accept rejection by them. Commitment gives the green light to a woman to truly give of herself.

## Women Want to Feel Appreciated

There is no more demonstration of love to a woman than by a man saying that he appreciates what she has done for him, their children or their home. Women need to feel appreciated in order to do more.

Women love to be told how wonderful they are at being homemakers or cooks or in their work. Women grow with praise and wither with constant criticism. In divorce proceedings women frequently complain that they are taken for granted, that they are never told that they are good at anything and that everything is expected of them. Women often can feel used and useless. For some women this can lead them to a spiral of depression.

Some women claim that, whilst men feel that they have a right to be appreciated, especially if they are the breadwinner, they seem to have no right to be appreciated as a wife or mother. Some say that husbands can cruelly say, 'I have been working all day, what have you been doing?' When they have been up at the same time and have been running around children all day and have continued to run around their husband after the children have gone to bed, such statements are irritating and inflammatory.

Dragon Women particularly feel this war between expectation and appreciation of the sexes. In the case of Dragon Women, they have chosen not to do any more because they claim they will not be appreciated if they do.

Whilst earlier in this book I have indicated the ways in

which women can encourage their men to appreciate them, the purpose of this chapter is to emphasise to men how important this can be to women.

Men must understand that for most women they do not expect men to actively participate in helping them with housework or looking after children, provided that they recognise and appreciate the contribution of the women themselves.

Many women complain that at the end of the day all they ever hear is how tired their partner is and never any recognition of how they might feel. If only he would just say, 'I know you must be tired and you are doing a great job', I would not feel so frustrated or unhappy or feel like throwing the dinner at him. Some women say that it is the arrogant failure of men to appreciate their input, which is the greatest friction between men and women in relationships today.

## Women Like Their Partners to Participate in Relationships with Them and Their Children

Women find men who love the children and help with them and make them feel a unit particularly alluring. Men who are affectionate to their wives and children find that they are generally shown huge amounts of affection in return.

If a woman knows that her partner is willing to help generally, this is very much appreciated and will help bond the relationship further. Women must remember that where a man does help she must appreciate his efforts. Men must realise that, if they never help around the home or with children, their partner will generally resent this and they will find in turn that their children can become distant.

Men must understand that, particularly with children, you get out what you put in. If you are cold and distant from your children, generally they will respond in this way towards you.

Women do not want coldness or distance, they want warmth, love and attention and so too do the children.

The purpose for a woman having a relationship is so that she can feel part of a unit. To a woman this is so that she can be reassured, seek comfort in that other person, make decisions with them and feel secure. So many women in divorce proceedings describe an innate feeling of loneliness in their relationship. They describe how they rarely talk with their partner, have little physical contact and lead virtually separate lives with separate interests and hobbies. It is always difficult to establish how or why the relationship has reached this point. However, what is clear is that women hate to feel lonely and unappreciated. They would far rather be on their own than face constant rejection within a relationship which they find demoralising and unfair. When a man boasts of how he has an open marriage where they both lead separate lives and they are both happy with this, normally, there is an unhappy and rejected woman sitting at home. Men must understand that to leave a woman lonely and abandoned within a relationship is very unfair. Mostly they will not understand, and many will say that when they have tried to discuss it, even in a non-critical way, they are cut off without explanation.

If you are unhappy in your relationship it is fairer to communicate this so you can work on the problem together rather than leaving your partner in isolated arctic conditions.

*All the lonely people, where do they all come from?*
– John Lennon & Paul McCartney

## Women Want to Talk

I have dealt at length in this book with why women like to talk. Put simply, men must learn to understand this and not to cut women off persistently.

## Women Like Men to Make Them Laugh

In surveys into what women found attractive about men after the initial allure, most women said that they adore men who are charismatic. Many claim that there is nothing more attractive than a man who makes them laugh. For a woman, laughing releases many different hormones. When a woman is happy, she is generally much more sexually receptive. Accordingly, when men are constantly miserable and negative, they will have the opposite effect on a woman. She will feel closed in and frustrated and will want to be as far away from him as possible. This is not to say that women will not stand by a man if he is depressed, because most certainly they will. However, they prefer men who make them laugh and can see the lighter side of life. This is why so often women can be attracted to men behaving badly, who do not take life seriously and with whom they can have fun. While they may be attracted to such men and have a fling with them, generally they will want to settle down with a man who is responsible. However, as women grow older, their craving for the lighter side of life rather than constant misery can encourage them to have affairs.

> *Laughter is a tranquilliser with no side effects.*
> – Arnold Glasgow

## Women Like to Receive Gifts as Evidence of Affection

Many women say that receiving gifts, however tiny, even a flower from the garden, can make them feel cared for and appreciated. Men must remember to do this as often as possible.

## Women Need Some Time for Themselves

Most women are not given the opportunity to do anything for themselves. They identify with being a wife, a mother or a worker, but not a person in their own right.

Men must allow their partners the occasional space to do their own things as well. It is so important that a woman does not neglect herself. Men should not make women feel guilty for wanting time for themselves, and if they do not want Dragon Women, should actively encourage them.

Perhaps for her next birthday you could consider buying her a weekend or a day at a health farm. She will really appreciate you for understanding her needs.

## Women Like Financial Security

As I have already indicated, women like security. As part of a woman's desire for security, she wants to feel that she has financial security. This does not mean that she will not understand genuine financial problems, but she will become extremely frustrated if her partner is financially irresponsible, especially if they have children. If he spends too much on himself, gambles, or gets involved in obvious loss-making enterprises, she will feel helpless, dreadful and insecure. Men must understand that women see such irresponsibility as an indication that their views and security are unimportant in their men's eyes. They will feel unloved as a consequence.

## Women Need Magic

Finally, what makes a relationship with a woman flourish and last? She needs a little bit of magic, the sense that a reservoir of treasures is still to be discovered in her mate and that the bond she shares with him will strengthen them as individuals and a unit in their work in the world.

To be happy, she must feel she can trust her partner, not

merely find him fascinating, but, even more than another person, she must trust her own ability to love. She must be allowed to be flexible, to learn from mistakes (her partner's and her own) and to enjoy the things that she discovers or is given without fear or recrimination. She needs understanding that she has the same freedom to love whom and what she pleases that her partner has himself, and that she has his respect just as he expects respect from her.

The sparkly aspects of a relationship – the ones which really keep people together and transform Dragon Women into peaceful, easily cherished, lifelong companions – are ephemeral, totally individual in nature and particular to the two individuals involved. They reinforce the love between them.

This love is impossible to precisely analyse or define because its qualities are infinite and unique to those who experience it together. It is, in essence, magic. It is a gift we are given and one we give to each other – something to be cared for and protected as one would the first shoots of a delicate plant.

Men often say that they do not understand what women require of them. I hope, having read this book, and particularly this last chapter, that men will be a lot wiser.

In the preceding pages, perhaps both men and women have discovered what might be holding them back from enjoying their relationships, so that they can grow and learn to love unhindered.

# TIPS FOR A HAPPY RELATIONSHIP

1. You should not give unsolicited advice to a man when it is not needed.

2. You should not be a space invader and should allow a man time to think things through for himself without nagging him out of your relationship.

3. You should not be over-critical; people grow with praise and shrivel with criticism.

4. You should praise the man you love.

5. You should not play mind games all the time; you must let him know what you want and be grateful for receiving gifts and holidays from him.

6. You should thank him for doing things around the home.

7. You should not immediately retaliate if he says something stupid.

8. You should try to have a loving and happy sex relationship, so don't reject his advances. If you are always too tired, then you must reassess your work schedule and what you really want from life.

9. Don't interrupt him when he talks. Let him finish his point, and don't make faces while he does.

10. Bring laughter into your relationship. Try to laugh hysterically together at least once a week. The happiest relationships are those where, even in adversity, you can laugh together. The world will not only seem a happier place; it will be one.

My conclusion after writing this book is that the message which needs to be broadcast is that if you don't communicate, you eradicate.

But always remember that, while love is grand, divorce is many many grand!

# List of Sources/Books to Help

*All About Menopause*
  Frank Murray, Abery Publishing Group

*All About Oxidants by Abery's FAQS series*
  Dr. Richard A. Passwater

*Beat PMT Through Diet*
  Maryon Stewart, Vermilion

*The Bluffer's Guide to Men*
  Anthony Mason, Oval Books, 1999

*Body Language, How to Read Others' Thoughts and Gestures*
  Allan Pease, Published by Sheldon Press, 1997

*Colin McDowell's Directory of 20th Century Fashion*
  Colin McDowell, Frederick Muller

*Coping with Stress*
  Dr. Donald Meichenbaum, Century

*Defeat Stress and Fatigue*
  Patrick Calford, Piatkus

*Introducing Feminism*
  Susan Alice Watkins, Marisa Rueda and Marta Rodriguez, Icon
  Books Limited

*Menstrual and Pre-Menstrual Tension*
  Jan Devries, Mainstream Publishing

*Men Are From Mars, Women Are From Venus*
  John Gray, HarperCollins

*Menopause*
  Dr. Miriam Stoppard, Dorling Kindersley Limited

*A New Guide to Rational Living*
  Albert Ellis, Wiltshire Book Company

*Relational Behaviour Therapy*
  Maxie Maultsby, Prentice Hall

*The Relaxation and Stress Reduction Work Book*
  Davis Eshelman and Mackay, New Harvinger Publications

*Saving the Situation*
  Julian Nettlefield, The Family Practice Press

*Secrets About Men Every Woman Should Know*
  Barbara de Angelis, Thorsons, 1998

*Sexuality, Sexual Behaviour and Pregnancy*
Kevin Hobbs, Ross Bramell and Catherine May, The British
Association for Sexual and Relationship Therapy

*Social Problems Cognitive Assessment From a Rational Emotive
Perspective*
Wendy Dryden, The Institute for RET, UK

*Super Nutrition for Healthy Hearts*
Dr. Richard A. Passwater

*Stress, Sanity and Survival*
Woolfolk and Richardson

*Structured Exercises in Stress Management*
Tubsing and Tubsing, WPP

*Thoughts and Feelings*
Mackay, Davis and Fanning, New Harvinger Publications

*The Ultimate Stress Handbook for Women*
Ursula Markham, Element

*30 Days to a Stress-Free Mind and Body*
Marina Callen and Suzanne Archer, William Caple

*The Vital Vitamin Book*
Boots

*Vitamin E Reduces Heart Disease Incidents*
Dr. Richard A. Passwater

*We Have to Talk*
Samuel Shem and Janet Murray, Basic Books, 1998

*Webb of Violence, A Study of Family Violence*
Jean Renvoize, Routledge and Kegan Paul

*What Your Father Couldn't Tell You and Your Mother Didn't Know*
John Gray, Vermilion, 1994

*Why Marriages Succeed or Fail and How You Can Make Yours Last*
Dr. John Gottman PHD, Simon and Schuster, New York

*Why Men Don't Listen and Women Can't Read Maps*
Allan and Barbara Pease, Pease Training International

*Women Are from Venus, Men Are from Hell*
Amanda Newman, Adams Media Corporation, 1999

*Women's Bodies, Women's Wisdom, the Complete Guide to Women's
Health and Well-being*
Dr. Christiane Northrup, Piatkus

*The Women's Book of Revenge*
   Christine Gallagher, Random House

*Women in Britain Since 1945*
   Jane Lewis, Blackwell Publishers

*Women's Health for Dummies*
   Pamela Moraldo, IDG Books Worldwide

*The Whole Woman*
   Germaine Greer, Anchor (A Division of Transworld)

*You Can Heal Your Life*
   Louise L. Hay, Eden Grove Editions

## Other Books to Help

*Defeat Stress and Fatigue*
   Patrick Calford, Piatkus

*Getting to Yes – Negotiating Agreement Without Giving In*
   Roger Fisher and William Galrey, Arrow

*Mars and Venus in Love*
   John Gray, Vermilion

*Conversation, How Talk Can Change Your Life*
   Theodore Zeldin Press

*It's Not What You Eat, It's Why You Eat It*
   Beechy Colclough, Vermilion

*Ten Steps to a Natural Menopause*
   Leslie Kenton, Vermilion

*How To Say No Without Feeling Guilty*
   Patti Breitman and Connie Hatch, Vermilion

*Families and How to Survive Them*
   Robin Skynner and John Cleese, Vermilion

*Stop Arguing, Start Talking*
   Susan Quilliam with Relate, Vermilion

*T'ai Chi*
   Alan Peck, Vermilion

*Alexander Technique*
   Chris Stephens, Vermilion

*The Self-Help Reflexology Handbook*
  Sonia Ducie, Vermilion

*One-Minute Stress Management*
  Dr. David Lewis, Vermilion

*The Sleep Solution*
  Dr. Nigel Ball and Nick Hough, Vermilion

*Too Good to Leave, Too Bad to Stay*
  Mira Kirshenbaum, Michael Joseph

*How to Stop Worrying and Start Living*
  Dale Carnegie, Vermilion

*Burn-out, The High Cost of Success and How to Cope With It*
  Dr. Herbert J. Freudenberger, Arrow

# Useful Telephone Numbers

Association of Personal Trainers, U.K.
  Tel: 0191 209 1031

The Body Control Pilates Association, London
  Tel: 020 7379 3734
  Tel: 0870 1690000

British Homeopathic Association, London
  Tel: 020 7935 2163

International Federation of Aromatherapy, London
  Tel: 020 8742 2605

London Marriage Guidance
  76A New Cavendish Street, London
  W1M 7LB
  Tel: 020 7580 1087

Motivation Plus Personal Trainers, London
  Tel: 020 8870 5808

The Nutrition Clinic
  1 Harley Street, London WCN 1DA
  Tel: 020 7935 4700

RELATE, U.K.
  Tel: 01788 573 241

Sleep Council, U.K.
  Tel: 0800 0187923

The Society of Teachers of the Alexander Technique, London
  Tel: 020 7351 0828

T'ai Chi UK, London
  Tel: 020 7407 4775

Women's Nutritional Advisory Service, U.K.
  Tel: 01273 487366